T0358206

Growth and Decline of American Industry

This short-form book presents key peer-reviewed research selected by expert series editors and contextualized by new analysis from each author on how the specific field has evolved.

The book features contributions on the history of government–business relations, regional and local business relationships, the development and formation of Silicon Valley and the rise and fall of the US machine tool industry after the Second World War.

Of interest to business and economic historians, this short-form book also provides analysis that will be valuable reading across the social sciences.

John F. Wilson is Pro Vice-chancellor (business and law) at Northumbria University at Newcastle. He has published widely in the fields of business, management and industrial history, including ten monographs, six edited collections and more than 70 articles and chapters. Most notably, his *British Business History, 1720–1994* is still being used in UK universities. He was also the founding editor of the *Journal of Industrial History* and coeditor of *Business History* for ten years.

Nicholas D. Wong is Vice-chancellor's Senior Research Fellow at Newcastle Business School, Northumbria University. His research areas cover historical organization studies and uses of the past, family business studies and entrepreneurship. He has published in *Business History, International Journal of Contemporary Hospitality Management* and *Entreprise et Histoire*. Nicholas won the John F. Mee Best Paper Award at the Academy of Management in 2018 for his contribution to the Management History Division.

Steven Toms has 15 years of senior management experience at Nottingham University as head of the undergraduate programme, chair of the teaching committee and research director and has been head of York Management School since 2004. Professor Toms's research interests cover the role of accounting, accountability and corporate governance in the development of organizations, particularly from a historical perspective. He is interested in perspectives that integrate financial models with economic and organizational theory and corporate strategy. Specific applications include business history, in particular cotton and other textiles trades, and capital markets and social and environmental accounting. He was editor of the journal *Business History* from 2007 to 2013.

Routledge Focus on Industrial History

Series Editor: John F. Wilson, Nicholas D. Wong and Steven Toms

This short-form series presents key peer-reviewed research originally published in the *Journal of Industrial History*, selected by expert series editors and contextualised by new analysis from each author on how the specific field addressed has evolved.

Of interest to business historians, economic historians and social scientists interested in the development of key industries, the series makes theoretical and conceptual contributions to the field, as well as providing a plethora of empirical, illustrative and detailed case-studies of industrial developments in Britain, the United States and other international settings.

Published titles in this series include:

Growth and Decline of American Industry
Case Studies in the Industrial History of the USA
Edited by John F. Wilson, Nicholas D. Wong and Steven Toms

Management and Industry
Case Studies in UK Industrial History
Edited by John F. Wilson, Nicholas D. Wong and Steven Toms

Banking and Finance
Case Studies in the Development of the UK Financial Sector
Edited by John F. Wilson, Nicholas D. Wong and Steven Toms

Growth and Decline of American Industry

Case Studies in the Industrial History of the USA

Edited by John F. Wilson,
Nicholas D. Wong and
Steven Toms

Routledge
Taylor & Francis Group

LONDON AND NEW YORK

First published 2020
by Routledge
2 Park Square, Milton Park, Abingdon, Oxon OX14 4RN

and by Routledge
52 Vanderbilt Avenue, New York, NY 10017

Routledge is an imprint of the Taylor & Francis Group, an informa business

British Library Cataloguing-in-Publication Data
A catalogue record for this book is available from the British Library

Library of Congress Cataloging-in-Publication Data
A catalog record for this book has been requested

ISBN: 978-0-367-02409-3 (hbk)
ISBN: 978-0-429-05902-5 (ebk)

Typeset in Times New Roman
by Apex CoVantage, LLC

Contents

Contributors

Steven W. Usselman is the H. Bruce McEver Professor of Engineering and the Liberal Arts at the Georgia Institute of Technology. He teaches and writes about technology and the American political economy since 1820. A past president of the Society for the History of Technology, he has received the Williamson Medal from the Business History Conference and the Hawley Prize from the Organization of American Historians.

Philip Scranton is University Board of Governors Professor Emeritus of History of Industry and Technology at Rutgers University. He directed the Hagley Museum & Library's Center for the History of Business, Technology and Society (1992–2012) and was editor-in-chief of the quarterly journal *Enterprise and Society* (Oxford University Press, 2007–2014). His publications include 16 books and 90 scholarly articles and chapters. His most recent studies are *Reimagining Business History* (with Patrick Fridenson, 2013) and *The Emergence of Routines* (coedited with Daniel Raff, Oxford, 2017). Presently, Scranton and Fridenson are developing "This Grave New World", a study analyzing postwar business practices in advanced capitalist nations, developing states and communist societies, intersecting with the rise of significant transnational institutions (under contract to Johns Hopkins). Concurrently, Scranton completed a monograph titled *Enterprise, Organization and Technology in China: A Socialist Experiment: 1950–1975*, published in 2019 by Palgrave Macmillan. He is continuing his research on socialist business practice, currently focusing on postwar Hungary, and to a lesser degree, on Poland.

Christophe Lécuyer is Professor of the History of Science and Technology and chair of the undergraduate major in business administration at Sorbonne Université. He is known for his research on the history of Silicon Valley and the history of high technologies. Among his publications are *Making Silicon Valley: Innovation and the Growth of High Tech* (MIT Press, 2006) and *Makers of the Microchip: A Documentary History of Fairchild Semiconductor* (MIT Press, 2010, in collaboration with David C. Brock). He has taught at MIT, Stanford University, the University of Virginia and the University of Tokyo.

Robert Forrant is the University of Massachusetts Lowell Distinguished University Professor of History. His recent publications include *The Great Lawrence Textile Strike of 1912: New Scholarship on the Bread & Roses Strike* (2014); *The Big Move: Immigrant Voices From a Mill City*, with Christoph Strobel (2011); and *Metal Fatigue: American Bosch and the Demise of Metalworking in the Connecticut River Valley* (2009). He is working on two new books: *Lowell: The Worlds and Histories of a New England Mill City* (University of Massachusetts Press) and *Interpreting Labor and Working-Class History at Museums and Historic Sites*, with Mary Anne Trasciatti (University of Illinois Press).

Introduction

*John F. Wilson, Nicholas D. Wong
and Steven Toms*

Purpose and significance of the series

The concept of the *Routledge Focus on Industrial History* series was motivated by the desire of the editors to provide an outlet for articles originally published in the defunct *Journal of Industrial History* (*JIH*). By using an extensive repository of top-quality publications, the series will ensure that the authors' findings contribute to recent debates in the field of management and industrial history. Indeed, the articles contained in these volumes will appeal to a wide audience, including business historians, economic historians and social scientists interested in longitudinal studies of the development of key industries and themes. Moreover, the series will provide fresh insight into how the academic field has developed over the past 20 years.

The editors believe that the quality of scholarship evident in the articles originally published in the *JIH* now deserve a much broader audience. The peer-reviewed articles are built on robust business-historical research methodologies and are subject to extensive primary research. The series will make important theoretical and conceptual contributions to the field and provide a plethora of empirical, illustrative and detailed case studies of industrial developments in the United Kingdom, the United States and other international settings. The collection will be of interest to a broad stratum of social scientists, especially business school and history department academics, because it provides valuable material that can be used in both teaching and research.

Building on the original *Journal of Industrial History*

The first edition of the *Journal of Industrial History* was published in 1998, with the aim of providing 'clear definitional parameters for industrial historians' and in turn establishing links between 'industrial history and theoretical work in social science disciplines like economics, management (including international business), political science, sociology, and anthropology'. Because it has been more than 20 years since its original publication, it is clear that the relevance of the *JIH* has stood the test of time. The original *JIH* volumes covered a diverse range of topics, including industrial structure and behaviour, especially in manufacturing and services; industrial and business case studies; business strategy and structure; nationalization and privatization; globalization and competitive advantage; business culture and industrial development; education, training and human resources; industrial relations and its institutions; the relationship between financial institutions and industry; industrial politics, including the formulation and impact of industrial and commercial policy; and industry and technology. The current *Routledge Focus on Industrial History* series will provide a cross-section of articles that cover a wide range themes and topics, many of which remain central to management studies. These include separate volumes: *Management and Industry*; *Industry in the USA*; *Banking and Finance*; and *Growth and Decline of American Industry*. Future volumes in the series will cover case studies in British industrial history; technology; and the cotton and textile industry. The *Routledge Focus on Industrial History* series will reframe highly original material that illustrates a wide variety of themes in management and organization studies, including entrepreneurship, strategy, family business, trust, networks and international business, focusing on topics such as the growth of the firm, crisis management, governance, management and leadership.

Volume Two: contribution and key findings

The second volume of this series is focused on the theme of industry in the United States, including articles that examine the development of a broad range of industries, covering the period 1880–2002. This volume will survey the debates related to a diverse range of industries that are central to the industrial and economic development of the USA, including American railroading and computing industries; the electronics industry of Silicon Valley; the Connecticut Valley machine tool industry; and the development of, and collaboration between, productive associations during American industrialization.

The first chapter, 'Trying to keep the customers stratified: government, business, and the paths of innovation in American railroading and computing', is a study by Steven W. Usselman that examines the topic of government–business relations in the USA. This chapter provides a unique perspective on the tension between business regulation and business management and the drive for efficiency and innovation in two industries, railroading and computing. Moreover, this study sheds fresh light on the strategy of industrial leaders and government to maintain a stratified customer base. In this chapter, Usselman was able to pinpoint the overlaps and similarities in the development of modern computing and railroading industries at the turn of the twentieth century. His detailed case studies uncover how both, in their own eras, were subject to similar difficulties in traversing the paths between innovation, productivity, integration and regulation.

The second chapter, 'Webs of productive association in American industrialization: patterns of institution formation and their limits, Philadelphia, 1880–1930' by Philip Scranton, homes in on micro-level, regional and local relationships between firms, sectors and institutions. He uses this framework to assess the networks and affiliations between regional trade associations and business institutions in Philadelphia during the late nineteenth century and the early twentieth century. Scranton examines how these networks were established and used to develop labour markets, manage products and influence politics. Adopting a novel approach borrowed from the disciplines of economic geography and economic sociology and applying institutional theory, he provides compelling evidence for the role of local trade associations in producing tangible sources of competitive advantage across local business networks. This study echoes the article of Andrew Popp (2000), which features in Volume One of the current series. Whereas Popp focused on the tension between competition and collaboration in the pottery industry of England, Scranton provides similar insights into the value of local networks and collaboration in Philadelphia, USA. This work foreshadows more recent studies on the value and function of local business networks that have emerged in the field of business history and management studies (Buchnea et al., 2018; Wilson et al., 2018; Maclean et al., 2017; Ostendorf et al., 2014).

The third chapter, by Christophe Lécuyer, 'Electronic component manufacturing and the rise of Silicon Valley', examines the development and formation of Silicon Valley. Combining the theories of Alfred Marshall and Michael Porter, Lécuyer provides a fresh perspective on the technological, socioeconomic and competitive dimension that contributed to the formation of Silicon Valley. Moreover, he sheds light on the processes that stimulate the development of industrial districts and how this encourages innovation and productivity. Perhaps most novel in Lécuyer's chapter is his coverage of entrepreneurial processes and innovation that supplemented the development of the industrial districts. This approach echoes a recent study by Wadhwani and Lubinski (2017) on entrepreneurial history that focuses on the creative processes that propel socioeconomic and cultural change.

The final chapter in the volume, 'Too many bends in the river: the decline of the Connecticut River Valley machine tool industry, 1950–2002', by Robert Forrant, addresses the question of what happened to the US machine tool industry after the Second World War. By focusing on the Connecticut Valley Region of western New England, Forrant is able to examine the key factors that contributed to the rise and fall of the machine tool and precision metalwork industry in the region. Considered an important area of US industry in business history literature, Forrant looks into the strategies adopted by American and Japanese firms in an attempt to avert the swift decline in the period after 1970. By developing case studies of three firms (Van Norman, Jones and Lamson and Bryant Grinding), Forrant provides insight into how US firms adopted numerical control techniques and how their relative success dwindled in comparison to the more innovative Japanese counterparts. The study concludes by detailing the decline of the industry in the US while foreign counterparts in Japan and Germany were able to prosper.

Conclusion

It is apparent from this brief review of the chapters that the second volume in the series makes important contributions to the field of industrial history in several ways. First, it provides a series of high calibre and unique studies in aspects of US industrial history that contributes to more recent debates on networks, industrial clusters, entrepreneurship and technological innovation. Second, the chapters shed light on studies that pioneered the link between history, business history and management studies in general. Finally, the volume provides strong historical case studies that can be used by students and researchers who are exploring issues related to the evolution and development of US management structures and industrial clusters and how they adapted and adjusted to periods of challenge, crisis and decline in response to increased international competition and technological advancements. The editors believe that this volume will not only provide a much wider audience for articles that link into a range of topical issues but also feed into debates in the wider social sciences. These are themes that will be developed further in subsequent volumes of the *Routledge Focus on Industrial History* series, highlighting the intrinsic value in republishing material from the *Journal of Industrial History* and ensuring that the articles contribute extensively to current debates.

References

Buchnea, E., Tilba, A., & Wilson, J. (2018). British corporate networks, 1976–2010: Extending the study of finance-industry relationships. *Business History*, 1–36.

Maclean, M., Harvey, C., & Kling, G. (2017). Elite business networks and the field of power: A matter of class? *Theory, Culture & Society*, 34(5–6), 127–151.

Ostendorf, J., Mouzas, S., and Chakrabarti, R. (2014). Innovation in business networks: The role of leveraging resources. *Industrial Marketing Management*, 43(3), 504–511.

Popp, A. (2000). Trust in an industrial district: The potteries, c.1850–1900. *Journal of Industrial History*, 3(1), 29–53.

Wadhwani, R., & Lubinski, C. (2017). Reinventing entrepreneurial history. *Business History Review*, 91(4), 767–799.

Wilson, J. F., Buchnea, E., & Tilba, A. (2018). The British corporate network, 1904–1976: Revisiting the finance-industry relationship. *Business History*, 60(6), 779–806.

Chapter 1

Trying to keep the customers stratified

Government, business, and the paths of innovation in American railroading and computing

Steven W. Usselman

Historians seeking to shed light upon the murky subject of government–business relations in America face a fundamental challenge. Somehow they must bridge the chaotic realm of politics, which gives rise to regulation, with an assessment of the long-term outcomes such regulation produces. This task has proved daunting, for participants and analysts alike. Those engaged in the politics of regulation must operate within the framework of the American party system. Though ideally suited to the business of campaigning for election and distributing favors, this system has posed severe obstacles for those who seek to provide the sort of sustained management demanded by the challenges of a mature industrial society. Those tasks have fallen on agencies operating at some remove from electoral politics. Students of regulation, meanwhile, find themselves similarly partitioned along disciplinary lines. Political scientists and political historians possess powerful instruments for evaluating voting behavior and interpreting electoral outcomes. Economists and economic historians, on the other hand, tend to concentrate their energies on the task of evaluating programmatic initiatives.[1]

The first generations of scholars who studied business regulation generally sidestepped this challenge. Presenting the history of regulation as a series of struggles between competing interests to control the course of legislation, they conflated political victories with regulatory outcomes. For the pioneering historians of the 1930s and 1940s, the establishment of regulatory agencies such as the Interstate Commerce Commission and the Federal Trade Commission provided a priori evidence that liberal democracy (The People) had triumphed over concentrated economic power (Big Business).[2] Later, a younger generation of historians turned this idea on its head. To these revisionists, the emerging government bureaucracies of the Cold War era appeared less like a source of countervailing power and more like unwarranted extensions of corporate influence into the public arena. Some influential figures, armed with detailed analyses of legislative history, went so far as to claim that the regulatory state had consciously been constructed by big business in a successful effort to close off more radical alternatives.[3] Even some historians less inclined to dismiss the achievements of the regulatory community acknowledged that government agencies tended over time to become captive to the industries they ostensibly oversaw.[4]

Arguments that business orchestrated the rise of federal regulation breathed new vigor into the study of business-government relations. One offshoot was a new spate of studies tracing the origins of regulatory statutes at the state and federal level. Many of these works emphasized the conflicting objectives of various interests in the business community.[5] By portraying business as something other than a monolithic entity, such studies blunted the force of the revisionist argument. The legislative arena now appeared less like a stage for grand conflict between opposing forces and more like a forum for complex negotiation among diverse interests. Legislation itself was read more as evidence of compromise than of triumph. Yet, however subtle their portrayals, these studies remained focused on political outcomes rather than on the actual social and economic ramifications of regulation.

Such was not true in the case of another critic of the revisionist position, railroad historian Albro Martin.[6] Suggestions that railroads may have benefitted from government regulation, or at least substantially muted its effects, struck Martin as wildly misguided if not preposterous. Hadn't the newly empowered Interstate Commerce Commission persistently denied requests by railroads for rate increases during the years leading up to World War I? For Martin, the issue was not whether government had established meaningful influence over business, but whether the public had reaped any genuine benefits as a result. Convinced that the public would have derived greater returns from an improved railroad system than from temporarily reduced rates, Martin argued that the refusal to grant the increases undermined the public interest by diverting capital away from railroading. Anticipating arguments that would grow increasingly influential in the seventies and eighties, this vehement defender of laissez-faire thus asserted that government interference had deprived society of the happy outcomes unregulated markets can produce. This sentiment would powerfully inform the movement toward deregulation, including the decisions in 1981 to break up AT&T and to discontinue antitrust action against IBM.

The attempt to hold regulatory performance up to a standard of economic efficiency has become a hallmark of many of the best recent studies of government–business relations. In his important study *Prophets of Regulation*, for instance, historian Thomas K. McCraw used the economic analysis of business historian Alfred D. Chandler as a yardstick against which to measure some of the key figures in the history of regulation.[7] Chandler had built a strong prima facie case that large business units can achieve extraordinary economies in certain types of industries, such as railroading. McCraw chided Louis Brandeis, who represented small shippers against railroads in the famed Eastern Rate Case of 1910, for failing to consider how consumers might ultimately have benefitted from lower prices had railroads received the income necessary to provide more efficient service. McCraw found more to admire in the thinking of Alfred Kahn, a guru of deregulation who introduced competition into the airline industry during the Carter administration. While acknowledging the power of market competition to drive out inefficiency, Kahn recognized that large business enterprises often faced distinctive cost calculations and other special circumstances that caused them to behave differently, but not necessarily less efficiently, than small firms. His reforms sought to introduce a brand of competition that acknowledged the distinctive features of large-scale enterprise and preserved the advantages it could provide, while keeping an eye on the welfare of consumers.

By emphasizing the interplay between economic structure, government policy, and consumer welfare, McCraw has assembled perhaps our most sophisticated sustained analysis of business regulation across the span of American history. His work helps reorient our thinking, shifting attention away from specific political struggles and focusing it instead on the persistent issue of economic performance. Yet despite its obvious contributions, one might well question whether this analysis captures the full complexity of the story. With its stress upon the Chandlerian framework, which accentuates the importance of high-volume throughput and economies-of-scale, McCraw's interpretation encourages us to frame our consideration of regulation narrowly in terms of efficiency and low prices. In recent years, business historians have questioned whether Chandler's account neglects important features of the corporate economy. Some have documented the persistent role of smaller firms and of economic sectors that fall outside the core of mass producers, settings where competition typically involves efforts to provide distinctive products rather than just low prices.[8] McCraw might well respond that such sectors have never attracted significant regulatory activity, precisely because market competition has functioned as an effective watchdog for consumer interests. But business historians have also come to appreciate that Chandler's portrayal of the corporate sector itself is not without flaws. His powerful interpretation is far too static. It does not account for the contining attention to innovation that has characterized most successful corporations of the twentieth century. Nor does it explain the continuing furor big business has generated in policy circles and in politics over matters that cannot, in the end, be reduced to questions of economic structure and prices.[9]

This paper seeks to meld this more dynamic conception of the corporation with the literature on government–business relations. It examines and compares the experiences of two "Chandlerian" industries – railroading and computing – during their first half century under federal regulation. The paper suggests that in both cases business managers and the regulatory community persistently wrestled with the difficult task of balancing the benefits of efficiency, which typically derived from routine and system, against the potential dynamism of innovation, which was typically aimed at meeting the needs of diverse customers.[10] In both industries, moreover, a key aspect of this struggle involved questions of institutional boundaries and markets. Through a combination of private actions and public policies, railroading and computing each evolved toward dualistic structures. One group of firms, often highly coordinated and perhaps even dominated by a clear industry leader, provided the basic platform. In the case of railroads, this platform consisted of the infrastructure of rails, stations, and shipping facilities as well as the rolling stock, which for technical reasons could not easily be disassociated from the infrastructure. In the case of computing, the basic platform exists not so much in the form of physical artifacts (though in its early years the industry did rely on tight physical coupling of central processors and peripheral devices into a technical system somewhat analogous to a railroad network), but as a set of rules governing logical design and programming (the latter known, suggestively, as the operating system).[11]

Both of these platforms offered ample opportunities for sustained improvement that would yield greater efficiency. Consumers would reap the benefits in the form of greater power (measured in tonnage transported or data processed) at lower cost. Many of those benefits resulted from relentless pursuit of standardization. Uniformity yielded economy, in the true sense of the word.

There was more to these industries, however, than sustained accomplishment along well-defined axes of limited criteria. For in each case, improvements in the basic platform also opened possibilities to perform entirely novel operations. In the case of computing, such novelties typically have occurred in the readily recognizable form of applications software. All of us who have experienced the steady stream of upgrades in our word processing programs over the past two decades well understand that technical change in computing involves new features rather than a mere increase in speed. The computer software and services industries have long emphasized product differentiation and customized installations.

Opportunities for novelty of this sort were not nearly so rich, of course, in the case of railroading. The basic platform was far more rigid, and though the rail lines achieved impressive productivity gains during the late nineteenth century, improvements such as steel rails and more powerful locomotives offered nothing like the extraordinary gains in cost-performance ratio that the solid state revolution has made possible in electronic computing.[12] Nevertheless, railroading did open the door for a wide range of novelty in the form of specialized transport services. The Pullman Company, operators of fleets of "palaces on wheels" featuring standard service of hotel quality, ranked fourth among the world's industrial corporations in 1912. Swift and Armour, whose meatpacking empires depended on special trains of refrigerated rail cars, occupied positions thirty-two and sixteen, respectively, in the same ranking. Westinghouse Air Brake, providers of specialized safety equipment deemed highly desireable by passengers and safety reformers, stood in the twenty-first position.[13] Railroads also serviced a number of express companies and tank car lines that were privately held.[14] All of these enterprises thrived at least in part by turning the utilitarian railroad toward a customized service; in that sense, they are analogous to software companies and service providers in the computer business.

To the extent that innovation of this sort involves customization, it necessarily exists in some tension with the pursuit of uniformity and routine that generally characterizes the behavior of those responsible for the basic platform. Not surprisingly, the push for novelty generally comes from outside, in the form of requests from particular consumers who bring distinct needs to bear upon the system. Providers of the basic platform often attempt to suppress such particularist interests and keep demand as homogenized as possible. It is no coincidence, for instance, that railroads permitted many of the service-oriented activities mentioned above to fall into the hands of outside concerns. Firms such as Pullman, Swift, and Westinghouse achieved success only after overcoming considerable resistance from railroads, which generally perceived the specialized services these businesses provided as too disruptive.[15] Evidence of similar tension runs through the history of the computer industry, where users have always been a primary source of innovation.[16] Dominant suppliers such as IBM and Microsoft persistently faced accusations that their standards placed unnecessary constraints upon those wishing to perform customized operations. Not coincidentally, both firms reluctantly gravitated toward so-called "open architectures" capable of facilitating a wide variety of specialized applications devised by numerous independent suppliers.

As these brief comments suggest, a key element in the ongoing trade-offs between uniformity and novelty involves the interface between platform providers and firms concerned with accommodating the specialized needs of particular consumers. Seldom has this boundary been sharply drawn. Technological interdependencies draw firms and consumers together in complex ways, and business strategies frequently converge. On many occasions, the critical interface has formed within the platform providers themselves, as their managers made trade-offs between the relative merits of pursuing further standardization versus the possibility of capturing greater returns by offering premium services. Even in these circumstances, however, the choices have always been made within a larger framework of public policy. Using instruments of rate regulation and antitrust, government has functioned as a watchdog, monitoring the critical boundaries that mediate the choices between uniformity-enhancing routine and product-differentiating innovation. Though government has hardly been unfailingly consistent or clear in its objectives, its focus has recurrently turned to the same fundamental challenge. Politicians and the regulatory community, like the firms they monitor, have struggled in their thinking and in their policies to conceive of the market not merely as a homogeneous mass seeking standard performance at lower cost, but as a collection of interests wishing to have their individual needs met through innovative service. They have tried, in other words, to keep the customers stratified.

Railroads

As George Miller observed a quarter century ago in his outstanding history of the Granger movement, the "railroad problem" of the late nineteenth century can be framed in terms of the fundamental break railroads made with previous forms of transportation such as roads and canals.[17] These earlier modes of transport had permitted a ready division of responsibility between companies that built and maintained the basic infrastructure and those that carried goods over it. In granting charters to canal and turnpike companies, governments routinely stipulated maximum rates that these firms could charge in return for their monopoly privileges. Such rates, which courts reviewed for reasonableness, were readily expressed on a per mile basis. Meanwhile the rates carriers could charge went unregulated, since governments believed competition among them would generate the most equitable prices. As long as the transport companies made their infrastructure available to all carriers, as their charters required, government could expect to see a vibrant competition that involved numerous variations in both price and service.

The interconnected nature of railroad technology broke down these neat boundaries. As providers of both infrastructure and carriage, railroads blended elements of regulated monopoly with those of intense market competition. Before the Civil War, when the railroad was largely perceived as a novel alternative that would bring increased competition to the business of transport infrastructure, the boundary problem did not pose severe difficulties. But as the network of tracks filled in and competition eroded the advantages localities had initially gained by constructing a rail line, the complex nature of railroading (and the intractability of the boundary problem) grew ever more apparent and pressing. Courts and state governments grappled for solutions, improvising as they went along. Sensitive to perceived discrimination resulting from local monopoly yet aware that railroad competition and costs involved a hopelessly complex set of variables, legislatures substituted vague long-haul, short-haul provisions for strict pro rata requirements. More importantly, they authorized commissions to adjudicate disputes involving particular localities and products. The process, highly contentious under any circumstances, grew all the more so under a system of federalism that at once multiplied and complicated the disputes.

The results were messy. By the late nineteenth century, published rate schedules showed a staggering array of classifications, and practices such as discounting and rebating (though ostensibly banned) no doubt introduced still greater variation into the rates actually charged. Individual charges reflected an indecipherable mix of custom, regulation, and competition. The schedules contained biases, with rates in the east generally favoring manufactured goods while those in the south and west subsidized agriculture.[18] Informed observers still argue whether rates favored long shipments over short, or vice versa. Yet for all its messiness, the system attempted to do precisely what I outlined at the start: to balance the advantages of uniformity and efficiency against the needs of a diverse customer base.

Despite the involvement of state commissions in ratemaking, primary responsibility for striking those balances remained decidedly in the hands of the railroads. Over the course of the late nineteenth century, they handled this task with a seeming bias toward efficiency. Under the influence of executives such as the Burlington's Charles Perkins, who spoke of railroad operations as "running the machine", railroads rapidly acquired the characteristics of utilities.[19] They rigorously pursued standardization and concentrated increasingly on efficiency through shipments of high-volume commodities, while letting companies such as Pullman, American Express, and Swift and Armour cater to the needs of more specialized customers. They increasingly turned responsibilities over to college-trained engineers who could substitute rigorous statistical analysis for individual judgement. By the 1890s, the Burlington's Perkins even stressed the importance of getting such men into the traffic department, the traditional province of customer-oriented salesmen known more for their ability to cut a deal than for their pursuit of efficiency. As historian Olivier Zunz has documented, these agents increasingly became extensions of the bureaucratized corporation, gathering its information in detailed traffic reports and enforcing its rules with employees and customers.[20] Meanwhile, lines increased their reach still further through expansion and merger, culminating in the 1890s with a wave of consolidation orchestrated by J. P. Morgan.

Whatever else these mergers may have accomplished, they left the resulting giants with a diversified portfolio of customers and rate schedules. Much like investors in mutual funds today, Morgan in effect hedged his bets, mixing so many winners and losers in the diverse market for railroad services that the variations came out a wash. Under these circumstances the distinctions among lines could then be boiled down to a few operational criteria, such as the number of ton-miles carried per capital invested. In effect, Morgan took demand (and consumers) out of the picture and assessed the health of a railroad according to a set of standard engineering measures. Capital could then flow to the few lines that best met those criteria.[21]

No sooner had Morgan's vision of railroading taken shape than it began to unravel, under pressure from two sources. One was the federal government. Beginning with its successful prosecution of the Northern Securities antitrust case in 1904, the Roosevelt administration moved to shape the railroad industry more actively. By 1910, the ICC had gained substantial authority over rate-setting, with the burden of proof in rate disputes now falling on the railroads. In the famous Eastern Rate Case heard that summer and fall, commissioners denied railroads a comprehensive increase. Over the next half-decade or so the ICC followed this comprehensive ruling with a series of judgements in more particular cases that generally favored shippers over railroads. These actions effectively turned Morgan's approach to demand back at him. Morgan had taken consumers out of play by making them part of a diversified portfolio; government policy enabled them to speak with a collective voice through the ICC. When the ICC proved a tough customer, it disrupted the ordered flow of capital into the industry that Morgan had desired.[22]

But government was not the only source of trouble for the railroads at the turn into the twentieth century. Even firms with ready access to capital, such as the mighty Pennsylvania, began painfully to realize that investments in additional capacity no longer yielded the expected returns in performance. With genuine alarm, Pennsylvania executives discovered in the opening years of the new century that the large new cars and locomotives they had purchased as part of a massive program of capital expenditures in fact carried far fewer ton-miles through the system than their predecessors.[23] The source of the problem lay not in the equipment itself, but in the congested yards that clogged the system. A surge in traffic with the economic recovery from the 1890s had placed unprecedented burdens on the system. More importantly, the *character* of the traffic had changed. The Pennsylvania and many other lines now carried an increasingly diverse range of high-value manufactured and agricultural products. Such goods moved in far more complex patterns than the commodities that had typified nineteenth-century shipments, and they often called for specialized services such as fast freight and less-than-carload lots. It took some time for managers at the Pennsylvania just to diagnose the new situation; the task of reorienting the firm's procedures and its corporate culture toward servicing these new demands would take still longer.

The job would prove all the more daunting, moreover, because it would have to occur in an unstable political atmosphere. At the Eastern Rate Case, railroads and the emerging regulatory community had effectively passed one another while moving in opposite directions. As railroads grappled with the changing character of demand, commissioners embraced the gospel of efficiency as espoused by Frederick Taylor and his momentary disciple, Louis Brandeis. Like Morgan before them, Brandeis and the commissioners held the railroads up to an engineering standard in order to determine their need for capital. Thus, railroads found themselves boxed into a discussion of efficiency at a moment when their performance was in fact growing less efficient as measured by conventional performance criteria. Their tentative efforts to shift the terms of argument foundered.[24]

In the decade that followed, the rhetoric of efficiency infused virtually every discussion of railroad regulation. All parties, including the railroads, couched their arguments in terms of efficiency.[25] Within that common language, however, railroads attempted to articulate an alternative vision of railroading that stressed differentiated customer service. Visitors to the Pennsylvania's exhibit at the 1915 world's fair in San Francisco, for instance, viewed movies of travels through especially scenic spots along its route. At previous fairs in 1904 and 1893, the line had featured its testing and research facilities, the source of its vaunted engineering standards.[26] The Pennsylvania also led the way in cultivating political support from shippers of high-value products, such as citrus growers and manufacturers.[27]

The experience of World War I obstructed and obscured this tentative effort to recast American railroading. Mobilization shifted traffic back toward the east-west patterns that had characterized the commodity flows of the late nineteenth century, while wartime objectives suffused railroading with a sense of urgency and patriotic self-sacrifice that imparted new power to the notion of disinterested engineering efficiency. Buoyed by the apparent success of wartime operations under federal control, an emboldened regulatory community – "engineers, commissioners, economists, and reformers", in Austin Kerr's typology, together with "many officials in the Railroad Administration" and "academics" – embraced national administration as a permanent solution to the railroad problem.[28] Sounding uncannily like Morgan nearly two decades before, these independent regulators had become the most vocal advocates of consolidation and engineering methodology, which they believed should now be applied to the rate-making process itself. Viewing competition as disruptive and wasteful, regulators embraced a rate-of-return approach that effectively reduced railroads to utilities offering undifferentiated service.[29]

Railroads and shippers resisted such thinking. Though willing to accept the notion of a guaranteed return on investment, railroads argued that they should retain any earnings in excess of those authorized by the experts. (Rather than have the ICC establish maximum rates, railroads would have had a Transportation Board set minimum earnings.) Significantly, railroads expressed their desire to compete for those excess earnings by providing service of high quality.[30] When wartime administrator William McAdoo lobbied for increased standardization of equipment, rail executives countered with recommendations "in favor of equipment designed to fit local conditions."[31] Railroads thus seemed prepared to function under a dual system, with a commodity-oriented business providing universal service and operating under conditions of a regulated utility, and a more competitive (and innovative) business aimed at meeting the demands of shippers willing to pay a premium for specialized services.[32]

Appeals such as these met with mixed response among railroad customers. Shippers believed service had suffered under wartime administration even as rates went up.[33] Most shippers, however, preferred simply to return to the system that had prevailed from 1910 to 1917, when a sympathetic ICC had consistently ruled in their favor and state commissions had continued to recognize their particular circumstances. Agricultural interests in the west and south and other shippers of commodities adamantly resisted any proposals to shift power away from the pre-war ICC to a transportation board.[34] Railroad proposals gained some support, however, among California citrus growers and others "whose business depended on fast transportation to distant markets."[35] Shippers and commercial interests in New England, Chicago, and other densely congested manufacturing districts likewise expressed some sympathy for the railroad position.[36]

The compromise legislation of 1920 neither embraced the strict efficiency orientation advocated by the regulatory community nor clarified the boundary issues along lines the railroads had suggested. The Act preserved the ICC as the supreme arbiter of relations between railroads and their customers while encouraging the agency to employ rate-of-return calculations and to exert a stronger coordinating hand over the industry. It thus loosely joined the pre-war, consumer-oriented system of rate regulation to administrative concepts appropriate to utilities such as electric power, which offered a far less differentiated product than transportation services. Few observers would characterize the resulting marriage as a happy one. Planning, coordination, and restructuring now occurred in the context of innumerable specific rate disputes, a realm where the ICC had always pursued what historian William R. Childs aptly calls a pragmatic approach, in which issues of equity and fairness traditionally took precedence. Those localized disputes, in turn, grew more complicated as they became enmeshed with the more comprehensive efforts to assess valuations and to calculate returns on capital. This was a recipe for ossification, not innovation.[37]

The timing could hardly have been worse, for the interwar years brought the widespread appearance of new means of mass transport – trucks and buses – that held the potential to radically reshape the transportation system. With its capacity to bring substantial pulling power right to the door of virtually any enterprise, the motor truck in particular promised to inject a strong dose of flexibility into the freight shipping industry. One could well imagine the decades of the twenties and thirties as a period of creative change, as transport providers melded railroads and trucks into a diverse system capable of serving a variety of customers. Indeed, several railroads took steps in that direction during the twenties when they created subsidiaries that operated fleets of motorized local delivery vehicles. Some even experimented with "piggyback" operations in which trailers were placed on railcars, then off-loaded and pulled by trucks to their final destination. A few pioneering truckers, meanwhile, used centralized sales and dispatching to introduce a measure of organization and routine into an industry that had initially been dominated by independent operators.

These tentative efforts to combine the virtues of system and coordination with the inherent flexibility of trucking soon foundered in a complex thicket of regulation. As independent and contract motor carriers began picking off some of the most lucrative trades and routes, they disrupted the convoluted rate schedules that had long formed an essential component of the regulated rail-based transport system. State governments, often acting with the encouragement of railroads, moved promptly to impose a measure of control over these practices. Exercising authority they possessed under the public purpose doctrines that underlay most railroad law or through the police powers they held over the state-funded highways, states implemented a variety of licensing provisions that stemmed some of the most aggressive competition. Over time, these measures sorted truckers into various classifications. Common carriers, who earned their livelihood strictly by transporting goods, were, like railroads, required by law to accept shipments from anyone willing to pay. At the other extreme were private operators, such as farmers, who drove their vehicles in conjunction with another line of work. Between these two fell a problematic third group, the contract truckers. Their ranks consisted of full-time operators who specialized in certain routes or in products that required special handling and equipment, such as milk, oil, produce, and lumber. These were just the sorts of high-return businesses that some railroads had begun to cultivate, and because contract carriers operated free of the burden of providing universal service, railroads and common carrier truckers felt disadvantaged in pursuing them. In their view, state licensing was in effect drawing inappropriate (and artificial) boundaries among transporters and between them and their customers. In an effort to break down those divisions, railroads attempted to have their wholly-owned subsidiaries who operated fleets of local delivery vehicles classified as contract shippers.

Predictably, the myriad of state regulatory provisions gave way in the nineteen thirties to federal regulation. Under pressure from many quarters, the ICC began holding hearings on the industry in 1932. Commissioner Joseph Eastman, who had been slow to recognize the significance of trucking, now came to envision a comprehensive restructuring of the transport system, with trucks, buses, and railroads each performing those functions most suited to them. Such a thoroughgoing rearrangement would require massive coordination, a task Eastman could not imagine entrusting to private firms in the marketplace. He pressed for government intervention on a scale that almost no other party to the discussions could tolerate. The idea of creatively melding transport modes thus gave way to a more preservationist mentality, in which trucking was seen as a competitive alternative to railroading that should be brought under a parallel mechanism of regulation. An act of Congress in 1935 extended ICC methods of control to the trucking industry, thus transforming an industry with low capital costs and easy entry into a public utility, with all the attendant difficulties.[38] "Transport" came increasingly to be conceived as an undifferentiated product offered to all consumers by parallel regulated systems, rather than as a highly differentiated product capable of servicing the demands of varied customers. This basic perception would persist until the seventies and eighties, when the deregulation movement broke down the divisions between transport suppliers, and firms dramatically redrew the boundaries of the industry.

Computing

The remarkable history of the American computer industry can perhaps best be understood as a sustained drive toward miniaturization punctuated by a series of technical compromises. Even the most casual observer could likely identify the main course of change. Sustained improvements in manufacturing technology have enabled producers of solid state componentry to cram ever more circuitry into smaller spaces for far less cost. Riding the natural trajectory of this "revolution in miniature", computer designers and programmers have produced machines of markedly increased capabilities and steadily diminishing expense.[39] Less appreciated, it seems, are the pauses along the way. For amid the ever advancing tide of miniaturization, the computer industry has periodically stabilized around a basic technological configuration involving standard componentry, logical design, and operating software. Each of these interludes has necessarily involved the same basic compromise. The potential for more rapid and more radical change at the technical frontiers of the industry has been sacrificed in exchange for the perceived benefits of standardization.

These critical compromises have typically been orchestrated by powerful firms that dominated the market for computing. For much of the industry's history, giant International Business Machines Company (IBM) performed this vital function. Capitalizing on abilities it had developed in the electromechanical era of data processing, IBM quickly garnered over 80% of the market for electronic computers, a position it held for over a quarter century.[40]

The key to IBM's success lay in the paramount importance of striking technical compromises. By their very nature, early computers presented designers with an extraordinary latitude that could easily prove disabling. Part of the complexity came from the fact that computers were hybrid assemblages of many components. A single installation involved not only choices of different subassemblies (printers, processors, storage devices), but also of different basic building blocks (resistors, tubes, semiconductors) that were themselves undergoing rapid development. Unlike virtually any other machine, moreover, computers had no single specific use. They could be altered to perform different tasks. Indeed, their expense made it essential that they possess such flexibility.[41] The tailoring process involved many things – the logical arrangement of circuits and switches, instructions encoded in language read by the machine's memory, input devices, storage, and printers (the latter three known collectively as peripherals). Over time, as innovations in magnetic and electronic storage reduced the cost of memory, more and more of this programming came to involve language.[42] But for many years switches and circuitry remained important tools for designers seeking to build flexibility into their systems. Peripherals have figured prominently throughout.

When government helped seed the market for computing by placing money in the hands of many potential users during the early Cold War, no company was better positioned to perform these essential balancing acts than IBM.[43] Its long experience with building and leasing electromechanical accounting equipment had not only made the firm familiar with the most sophisticated calculating techniques of the day; it had also fostered a set of abilities that ideally suited the challenges of computing. The mechanical experts and inventors who had designed new electromechanical accounting equipment took basic components and arranged them in complex machines that were leased to customers and maintained by IBM in the field. Working in collaboration with their customers and their assemblers, the field force tailored the machines to perform a variety of specialized tasks. Within the plant and the corporate office, manufacturing experts looked always for ways to build standardization into the machines while retaining sufficient flexibility to meet the demands of each user. IBM had learned how to strike a balance between novelty, which generated revenue, and standardization, which produced economy.[44]

As IBM entered the field of military-scientific computing, its tradition of pursuing many markets and its capacity to transfer lessons from one to another paid great dividends. The firm never lost sight of the potential applications for computing among its established business customers and consistently sought to exploit possible connections between the military and commercial sectors of the market. Because IBM ended up with development efforts aimed at all segments of the market, moreover, it was then in a position to see and feel pressures from what would soon emerge as the central recurrent dynamic force in the computer industry: the convergence of machines designed for one market with those designed for another as the availability of new memory increased programming capacity and as changes in componentry improved processing power. From the mid-fifties on, this issue continually created problems within IBM, as its machines competed with one another in the marketplace and its development efforts overlapped. Steps taken during this period eventually culminated in System/360, a single line of computers introduced in April 1964 that replaced all other IBM machines, ran the same programs, and contained solid state circuits of the same standard design manufactured from scratch entirely within IBM. No other product announcement would have a more profound affect on the computer industry – at least until the coming of the personal computer.[45]

The key to success with System/360 remained not simply to master components, but to strike balances between componentry, logical design, and markets. In building a new facility for manufacturing basic components, for instance, IBM struck a fundamental compromise. It chose not to develop the new integrated circuits and instead concentrated on building a production line of great flexibility that could readily respond to shifts in demand and keep track of design changes. True to its heritage, even as it moved into extraordinarily capital intensive process manufacturing, IBM did not want to sacrifice the flexibility it had come to rely on as an assembler of customized machines. Though System/360 is often lauded as bringing a high degree of order to the market by consolidating IBM's offerings in a few standard models, in reality the system included machines of numerous variations.

Though the approach to computing embodied in System/360 emerged from the private pursuit of profit by a firm operating in a largely unregulated environment, the product achieved such phenomenal success that IBM's strategy in effect constituted a national policy toward computing. That was certainly the view from abroad, at least.[46] Throughout the sixties and seventies, governments in most industrialized countries scrambled to encourage firms that would mimic IBM and keep the American colossus at bay. Americans themselves, secure in their position of world leadership, pursued a less interventionist strategy. Government actually reduced its role as a procurer of computing technology and instead came to rely almost wholly upon the tools and traditions of antitrust to monitor the industry. IBM, with its enormous share of the market, presented an obvious target. From the time the firm entered into a consent decree with the Justice Department in the 1930s until a thirteen-year lawsuit against it was deemed "without merit" in 1982, IBM attracted virtually continual attention from antitrust investigators and the courts. These proceedings chastened IBM, but they ultimately left the firm intact and effectively certified the paradigm of computing it had long pursued.[47]

In reaching this series of antitrust judgements, Americans struck basically the same compromise that had characterized so many of IBM's own decisions regarding computing. They weighed the benefits of standardization against the potential for further innovation. Influential figures in the regulatory apparatus viewed the computer giant as a useful intermediary between a rapidly changing technology and a market of consumers who were anxious to put that technology to a variety of uses. By controlling such a large share of the market for central processors and peripherals, IBM instilled a measure of stability into an industry that well could have foundered in a sea of conflicting, incompatible approaches. It provided the emerging semi-conductor industry with demand for standardized componentry, and it enabled programmers to develop a few basic languages and then allocate their energies toward developing specific applications. A consent decree of 1956 sought to ensure that IBM would perform a similar function for manufacturers of punched cards and peripherals. The decree required IBM to sell as well as lease its products and to allow consumers to purchase parts of their systems from competitors.[48] In effect, the Justice Department positioned IBM as a broker or common carrier for component and peripherals manufacturers and for applications programmers, much as the FCC had done with network broadcasters.[49]

The government's strategy was not without risks. A firm with IBM's market power could potentially exert pressure on suppliers and customers and effectively dictate technical choices for the industry as a whole. For a decade after the consent decree, competitors made little headway in getting their peripherals attached to IBM systems. Some industry observers complained that banks and insurance companies unduly influenced IBM and kept it from aggressively pursuing applications and approaches to computing that would have suited more creative customers. By the early sixties, sophisticated scientific users had begun to look elsewhere for computers. At about the same time, many within the technical press roundly criticized IBM for not using the new integrated circuitry in its System/360 computers. Several potential customers expressed disappointment that the new series of machines did not offer better time-sharing capabilities. Such criticisms suggested that IBM had struck a balance that unnecessarily impeded innovation. Its sometimes frantic efforts to make up the deficiencies did little to dispel that impression or to discourage the Justice Department from launching a new investigation.[50]

The major antitrust suit that resulted, announced in January 1969, serves as vivid testimony to the seriousness with which the American government pursued the course of compromise. Viewed from an international perspective, the suit appeared preposterous. At the time it was launched, governments in almost every advanced industrial nation were busily trying to imitate IBM.[51] The decision to prosecute can only be understood within the context of what was a watershed moment in American political economy, when influential figures in the regulatory establishment embarked on a fundamental reexamination of the brokering agreements that had characterized much of American economic policy. The case against IBM marched in almost exact parallel with that against AT&T, each reaching its denouement on a single afternoon in 1982.

The contrasting outcomes of those cases prompted some to see a conspiratorial tradeoff, in which a probusiness administration achieved "compromise" by pardoning one guilty party while publicly sacrificing another. But the two judgements actually reflected the same basic philosophy. In each case, government officials had sought ultimately to assure themselves that leading firms had not abused their power in ways that stifled innovation and threatened the good outcomes that market competition could achieve. This was the common thread of the deregulation movement. Though proceedings such as those against AT&T and IBM necessarily focused on particular behaviors and complaints, the overarching consideration for the Department of Justice in 1982 was whether the government was protecting monopoly or not. Without government protection, Assistant Attorney General Baxter thought, monopoly could not exist unless it was efficient and innovative. Measured on that basis, the contrasting moves of the Justice Department were consistent and prescient as well. For whatever one might think of the merits of the case against IBM or of the paradigm of computing the company had advanced, no one could argue that the computer industry lacked dynamic forces of change during and after the period the lawsuit was contested. Technology-based competition would accomplish for computing what Justice Department lawyers had done for telephony.[52]

The fundamental source of change in computing during the seventies and eighties remained the same as before. Continual refinement of solid state production technology made available processors of much higher speed and also dramatically increased the memory and storage capacities of computing systems. Increased capacities gave programmers much greater latitude. Instead of devoting the lion's share of their energies to conserving processor time, programmers increasingly could focus their efforts on making computers receive data in different forms, manipulate it in various ways, and present the results in more comprehensible fashion. Data-processing continued its metamorphosis into information-processing.

Much of this transformation occurred within the basic paradigm IBM had established with System/360. Its modular design, in combination with new systems applications such as time-sharing, opened huge opportunities for equipment manufacturers to concentrate on building lower-cost versions of common components such as printers and terminals. The 1956 consent decree had at last begun to bear fruit. Additional competition came from dynamic new firms such as Digital Equipment Company and Wang Industries. Taking advantage of the plummeting cost and shrinking size of components, these start-up companies built "mini-computers" tailored to serve particular types of users.[53]

Meanwhile, miniaturization unleashed an alternative path of innovation that fell entirely outside the IBM paradigm and the realm of institutional users it served. Individual enthusiasts began to patch together one-of-a-kind computers of limited capacity. Infused with a strong anti-institutional ideology and renegade spirit, these hackers brought the vision of a "home computer" into reality.

The era of the unshackled amateurs did not last for long, however, as firms such as Apple Computer and IBM soon imposed a degree of order on the personal computer market. Though Apple portrayed itself as David to IBM's Goliath, it actually filled a role quite analogous to that Big Blue had performed in the postwar computer industry. Rather than offer a stripped-down, expandable kit that customers could assemble and refine themselves, Apple sold a standard machine that included its own monitor, disc drive, and keyboard. The company also provided several basic software packages. Many enthusiasts complained that the firm made overly conservative choices and did not press the technical boundaries of microcomputing. But compared to virtually any other supplier of home computers, Apple projected an image of stability, and as a result it enticed large numbers of less technically inclined customers into the domain of the hackers. Apple's revenues soared from three-quarters of a million dollars in 1977 to just under a billion dollars in 1983. This success helped spur IBM to launch a crash program to develop a micro-computer of its own. Its PC, introduced in 1981, immediately captured 26% of the market. The impact of the PC went well beyond IBM's own sales, moreover, because the product's modular design and extensive use of licensed components left other manufacturers free to produce clones that accounted for another fifty percent or more of the market. In effect, IBM with the PC repeated its experience with System/360 in mainframe computing, only in fast forward. Drawing on its market presence and its capacity for technical compromise, IBM provided a platform that helped rapidly transform the desktop computer into a standardized mass-produced commodity, then watched as low-cost competitors undercut it in the marketplace.

Within a short time of its decision to drop the antitrust case, then, the Justice Department could feel satisfied that the computer industry had entered a period of vibrant economic and technical competition. But though growing commodification had diminished IBM's prominence, it had by no means eliminated the need for the technical balancing act that had long characterized the computer industry and its leading firm. Computers remained machines of indeterminate purpose. Indeed, as they grew more commonplace and came into the hands of a more diverse population, the possibilities of what they might do continued to expand. Yet so too did the chances increase that programmers would become mired in a myriad of incompatible approaches. Meanwhile, the drive toward miniaturization continued apace, keeping designs in perpetual flux. Within the separate but parallel realms Apple and IBM had created, designers and programmers thus still needed to strike compromises and achieve a balance between standardization and customization.[54]

By the mid-eighties, that balancing act had come to focus on two fundamental issues – the design and production of the microprocessor, and the basic operating language. With Apple, both were proprietary; in the case of the PC, they were shaped respectively by Intel and Microsoft, the firms IBM had chosen as its original suppliers.[55] In a move that clearly heralded its prominence in hardware production, Intel in the early nineties began advertising directly to consumers. It gave its processors catchy names and insisted that machines containing its processors carry an "Intel Inside" sticker. Meanwhile, Microsoft had grown more profitable than IBM. As owner of the MS-DOS and Windows programs, it supplied the essential gateways through which most users gained access to their personal computers.

Like IBM in the early mainframe computer industry, these powerful firms established a degree of uniformity in the essentials of computing without closing off the potential for further development. They continued to introduce new generations of processors and operating systems that placed greater computing power at the hands of individual consumers. Their influence and market power gave suppliers of memory, printers, and monitors confidence to pursue techniques of mass production. Most importantly, software writers could proceed with some assurance that their work would find a broad market and not be rendered obsolete by subsequent changes in basic hardware or in the basic operating system. As a result, the micro-computer industry sustained a vibrant competition to develop new applications, and computers came to perform a much broader array of functions.

As with IBM before them, these dominant firms attracted virulent criticism. Competitors and some consumers accused them of wielding their market influence unfairly to close off technical alternatives. Critics of Microsoft sought antitrust action that would have forced the company to sever all connections with hardware suppliers and banned it from the applications business, in effect leaving the firm to operate as a common carrier for specialized software programs written by others. A settlement announced in the summer of 1994 stopped short of either action. As it had in the case of IBM, the Justice Department determined that Microsoft managed to provide a healthy stability without stifling development. When a federal judge overturned the settlement in early 1995, the Justice Department and Microsoft joined in an unlikely alliance that successfully appealed the decision. (As noted below, they have subsequently renewed their hostilities, as Justice Department officials have accused Microsoft of violating the 1994 agreement by bundling its operating system with its internet browser.)

Critics made even less headway against Intel, which clearly faced intense competition from numerous domestic and foreign manufacturers.

Indeed, during the late eighties government had grown so concerned about foreign competition that it had fostered Sematech, a cooperative effort among American semiconductor producers. Policymakers hoped Sematech would promote compromise in design and enable firms to capture the economies of standard production. This cooperative effort passed out of existence in 1994, and responsibility for striking balances between the economies of volume production and the added value of specialized design again became the exclusive province of private firms operating in a competitive, oligopolistic marketplace.

The Sematech venture and the Justice Department settlement with Microsoft demonstrate both the continuing importance of technical compromise to the computer industry and the sustained commitment of public policymakers to promoting it.[56] Though each left the dominant firms largely unaltered and free for the moment to compete without significant restriction in the marketplace, they also left little doubt that all aspects of computing would continue to operate under the watchful eye of the government. The Justice Department prohibited Microsoft from purchasing a competitor but voiced no public objections when IBM bought the Lotus software development firm for a price in excess of three billion dollars. In restricting a horizontal combination involving the dominant firm while tolerating a vertical integration on the part of a large competitor, the government's antitrust lawyers again embraced oligopoly as the best means of maintaining a climate of vigorous competition at the frontiers of the industry.

Summary and prospects

In juxtaposing these analyses of computing and railroading, it is perhaps tempting to label one a success and the other a failure, or to interpret the contrasting outcomes of the joined stories as a brief against government involvement. My hope is the comparison yields insights less stark. The two stories illuminate common, persistent challenges that have occupied private firms and public entities in a variety of industrial contexts for over a century. Seldom have those challenges called forth clear, unambiguous responses. The situations described above entailed genuinely difficult trade-offs among many interested groups with legitimate claims. To the extent the choices involved the possible course of subsequent innovation, an endeavor fraught with uncertainty, they neccessarily entailed an element of indeterminancy. Boundary-drawing involved judgement, and we cannot assess the outcomes against some absolute standard of performance.

Nor can we presume that the effort to draw boundaries necessarily produced less advantageous outcomes than those that would have occurred in the absence of government intervention. Though government intervened more actively and persistently in the case of railroading, it also significantly influenced the boundaries in computing. The apparently divergent results in these two cases, moreover, owed as much to differences in the nature of the basic technology as to particular policies. Railroading lacked the inherent flexibility of electronic computing. Government missed opportunities to encourage greater flexibility and may in some respects have compounded the rigidity, but the task it confronted was enormously difficult. At the time the federal government became involved in the industry, railroads provided many Americans with their only easy access to markets.

As we approach the end of the twentieth century, these basic contrasts between railroading and computing have narrowed. Railroading now exists as one alternative among many, and government has responded by redrawing substantially the boundaries in which it operates. Meanwhile, the fruits of continuing miniaturization and further economies of manufacture in electronics have driven computing toward a grand convergence with communications technologies, which are now all grounded in the common underpinnings of digital technology. In the process, computing has acquired an indispensability not unlike that which characterized railroading at the end of the nineteenth century. In a contest reminiscent of transportation history, builders of infrastructure such as AT&T and the cable television providers vie with carriers such as Microsoft and the entertainment networks to gain influence over an integrated system capable of providing diversified products to consumers. This jockeying takes place under the vigilance of a regulatory community madly struggling to reassess boundaries. It is no coincidence that the most recent bone of contention between the Justice Department and Microsoft has involved the browsers used to negotiate the internet, because the internet shows signs of emerging as an indispensable communications tool not unlike the telephone and the railroad at the turn into the century. Does the browser constitute the critical interface between consumers and an essential public utility? Will those who operate the browser accommodate the specialized needs of all consumers? In posing such questions, the Justice Department demonstrates that the ongoing effort to secure innovation and stability, achieved through a mix of market mechanisms and public policy, apparently remains a hallmark of American political economy even in the era of interconnectedness. The struggle to keep the customers stratified continues.

Steven W. Usselman postscript

This chapter originated with a presentation given at the Business History Conference (BHC) in Glasgow on July 4, 1997 (American Independence Day). This was the first time that the BHC had met outside of North America. Although I had crossed the Atlantic, my talk remained firmly grounded in the US and its distinctive political economy. It brought together, for the first and only time, my two principal fields of research: railroading and computing.[57] I tried to suggest how government policy and private enterprise in these two systems-based industries had traced similar paths. The ongoing jostling among various private and public interests in each setting had betrayed a common purpose. In both industries, the parties had grappled with the inherent challenge of balancing the efficiency of standardization and uniformity against the desire to meet the varied desires of multiple consumer interests. The situations, I suggested, had not boiled down to a simple choice between public or private ownership and control. Rather, they had involved a mix of policies – rate regulation, common carrier provisions, intellectual property law, licensing provisions, and antitrust – intended to promote the establishment of stable platforms (plural) that would provide sufficient uniformity and compatibility while accommodating multiple consumers.

The talk was unapologetically presentist. Although I drew on rich bodies of primary and secondary research on each industry, my remarks (and the subsequent chapter) built explicitly toward a pregnant policy issue of the day: Microsoft Corporation's attempt to leverage its dominant position in PC operating systems – a classic platform – by tying specific applications programs to that system and blocking applications supplied by third parties. The particular application in question was something most computer users at the time were only dimly aware of, if at all: an Internet browser (known as Netscape). Both US and EU antitrust officials sought to end the practice – a move I likened to earlier suits against IBM (a firm that had handed Microsoft the PC operating system business) and to the long history of US regulation in telecommunications and railroading.[58]

Returning to this piece nearly a quarter-century later, it strikes me as at once terribly quaint and extraordinarily prescient: quaint because the halcyon days of Microsoft and Netscape seem wildly removed from today's world of tech giants spawned by the Internet and the devices used to access it. As with railroading in its heyday, these large corporations include not only the network operators themselves but, more significantly, firms that have built strongholds by using the new infrastructure.

These latter-day equivalents of Pullman, Swift, and Sears include Amazon (founded in 1994 as an online bookstore), Netflix (1997, as a video streamer), Google (1998, as a search engine), Facebook (2004, as a social media site), and Apple (which introduced its iPhone in 2007, a decade after being saved from extinction by an infusion of cash from Microsoft's Bill Gates, in an ill-advised move intended to relieve anti-trust pressures).

Yet it was prescient too, because these tech giants have attained such prominence largely through their ability to leverage control of widely used platforms (sometimes still overtly referred to as operating systems). As they have battled to gain a more secure foothold in the lives of their customers – now tellingly referred to as users – they have increasingly become targets of regulation themselves. A call for "net neutrality", which aims to preserve the Internet as a common carrier open to all without privilege, remains a persistent feature of American politics. It echoes with concerns about special privileges and insider deals such as rebates that railroads once granted to large customers. Meanwhile, antitrust officials on both sides of the Atlantic maintain close watch over the new giants. Voices from across the political spectrum sound warnings about their invasiveness and power. This morning's *New York Times* contained an editorial by one of Facebook's founders, calling for the breakup of the company. The firm's CEO, Mark Zuckerberg, declared a preference for regulation.[59] Either way, the old political economy stirs. Where it will lead, in a world where global firms know their customers better than the customers know themselves, I would not hazard to guess.

Notes

1 My reading of the literature is heavily influenced by the trenchant essays in Richard L. McCormick, *The Party Period and Public Policy: American Politics from the Age of Jackson to the Progressive Era* (New York, 1986).
2 For an example of the institutionalist approach of particular relevance to this paper, see I. L. Scharfman, *The Interstate Commerce Commission: A Study in Administrative Law and Procedure*, 5 vols (New York, 1931–1937).
3 The classic statement is Gabriel Kolko, *The Triumph of Conservatism: A Reinterpretation of American History, 1900–1916* (New York, 1963) and *Railroads and Regulation, 1877–1916* (Princeton, 1965). See also James Weinstein, *The Corporate Ideal in the Liberal State, 1900–1918* (Boston, 1968).
4 This was a major theme of Thomas K. McCraw, "Regulation in America: A Review Article", *Business History Review* 49 (1975): 159–183.
5 K. Austin Kerr, *American Railroad Politics, 1914–1920* (Pittsburgh, 1968); George H. Miller, *Railroads and the Granger Laws* (Madison, 1971);

Edward A. Purcell, Jr., "Ideas and Interests: Businessmen and the Interstate Commerce Act", *Journal of American History* 54 (1967): 561–578; and Richard H. K. Vietor, "Businessmen and the Political Economy: The Railroad Rate Controversy of 1905", *Journal of American History* 64 (1977): 47–66. The most careful works in the politics of regulation had in fact always stressed the multiplicity of interests that typically influenced legislation. See for example Richard Hofstadter, *The Age of Reform: From Bryan to F.D.R.* (New York, 1955) and especially Arthur S. Link, *Woodrow Wilson and the Progressive Era, 1910–1917* (New York, 1954).

6 Albro Martin, *Enterprise Denied: Origins of the Decline of American Railroads, 1897–1917* (New York, 1971) and "The Troubled Subject of Railroad Regulation in the Gilded Age", *Journal of American History* 51 (1974): 339–371.

7 Thomas K. McCraw, *Prophets of Regulation* (Cambridge, Mass., 1984). See also his "Rethinking the Trust Question", in Thomas K. McCraw, ed., *Regulation in Perspective* (Cambridge, Mass., 1981), pp. 1–55. The starting point for Professor Chandler's vast writings on business history is Alfred D. Chandler, Jr., *The Visible Hand: The Managerial Revolution in American Business* (Cambridge, Mass., 1977).

8 For a recent analysis, see Philip Scranton, *Endless Novelty: Specialty Production and American Industrialization, 1865–1925* (Princeton, 1997).

9 These thoughts on the static nature of Chandler's analysis are influenced by Naomi Lamoreaux and Louis Galambos, "Understanding Innovation in the Pharmaceutical Industry", a paper written for the conference Understanding Innovation at Johns Hopkins University, June 6, 1997. Professor Chandler has already begun to respond to this challenge with his current project, *Paths of Learning: The Evolution of High Technology Industries*.

10 For an excellent introduction to American political economy that raises precisely this dichotomy, see Louis Galambos and Joseph Pratt, *The Rise of the Corporate Commonwealth: United States Business and Public Policy in the 20th Century* (New York, 1988).

11 My use of the terms "platform" and "system" perhaps needs some elaboration, given their centrality to my arguments here. My reading of the literature on computing suggests that the terms coexist comfortably in that domain. This seems less true in the case of railroading, which many scholars, including me, have aptly characterized as a system. One liability of the systems approach, however, is that it tends to exaggerate the degree of rigidity in the subject being studied. I have chosen the term "platform" in a conscious attempt to counter that tendency. For my thinking on systems analysis and the railroads, see Steven W. Usselman, "Changing Embedded Systems: The Economics and Politics of Innovation in American Railroad Signaling, 1876–1914", in Jane Summerton, ed., *Changing Large Technical Systems* (Boulder, CO, 1994): 93–116.

12 On productivity improvements in railroading, see Albert Fishlow, "Productivity and Technological Change on American Railroads, 1869–1900", in National Bureau of Economic Research, *Output, Employment, and Productivity in the United States after 1800* (New York, 1966), pp. 583–646. One should be cautious about exaggerating the contributions of computing to productivity. Although observers of the industry are fond of citing the

extraordinary sustained increase in processing speed and corresponding decrease in cost, speed is a technical measure that by no means corresponds directly with improvements in economic productivity. Writers of application software have found ways to absorb much of the increase in speed without noticeably advancing the productivity with which we perform information processing and other tasks.

13 This data comes from Leslie Hannah, "Marshall's 'Trees' and the Global 'Forest': Were 'Giant Redwoods' Different?", in Naomi R. Lamoreaux, et al., eds, *Learning By Doing in Markets, Firms, and Countries* (Chicago, 1999), pp. 253–86. The list of the top 100 industrial enterprises also includes American Car and Foundry (50th), American Locomotive (79th), and Baldwin Locomotive (88th). A third meat packer, Cudahy, ranked 97th.

14 Peter Z. Grossman, *American Express: The Unofficial History of the People Who Built the Great Financial Empire* (New York, 1987) and "Golden Silence: Why the Railroad Express Chose Not to Incorporate", *Business and Economic History* Second Series, 21 (1992): 300–6.

15 On Pullman, see Stanley Buder, *Pullman: An Experiment in Industrial Order and Community Planning, 1880–1930* (New York, 1967). On railroad resistance to meatpackers, see Mary Yeager, *Competition and Regulation: The Development of Oligopoly in the Meat Packing Industry* (Greenwich, CT, 1981). On Westinghouse, see Steven W. Usselman, "From Novelty to Utility: George Westinghouse and Business of Innovation in the Age of Edison", *Business History Review* 66 (1992): 251–304.

16 JoAnne Yates, "Co-evolution of Information-Processing Technology and Use: Interaction between the Life Insurance and Tabulating Industries", *Business History Review* 67 (Spring 1993): 1–51.

17 Miller, *Railroads and the Granger Laws.*

18 Kerr, *American Railroad Politics*, pp. 8–11.

19 C. E. Perkins, "Memorandum on Organization", n.d. (ca. 1880), Papers of the Chicago, Burlington, and Quincy Railroad, Newberry Library, Acc. 3P6.36. Usselman, "From Novelty to Utility".

20 Olivier Zunz, *Making America Corporate, 1870–1920* (Chicago, 1990), pp. 37–66.

21 For an example of the Morgan approach at work, see Stuart Daggett, *Railroad Reorganization* (Cambridge, Mass., 1924).

22 In addition to the works of Martin and Kerr cited above, see Stephen Skowronek, *Building a New American State: The Expansion of National Administrative Capacities, 1877–1920* (Cambridge, Mass., 1982) and Morton Keller, *Regulating a New Economy: Public Policy and Economic Change in America, 1900–1933* (Cambridge, Mass., 1990), pp. 43–55.

23 This assessment of the situation at the Pennsylvania is based on materials in the Association of Transportation Officers Papers, Pennsylvania Railroad Papers, Hagley Museum and Library, Wilmington, Delaware (hereafter, ATO Papers).

24 McCraw, *Prophets of Regulation*, pp. 80–94 and Martin, *Enterprise Denied.*

25 This is a recurrent theme in Kerr, *American Railroad Politics.*

26 On these exhibits, see ATO Papers.

27 Such steps served a decidedly political purpose, of course. In his authoritative account, Austin Kerr shows how the rhetoric of service often melded

with the gospel of efficiency, especially when joined to the concept of public service. But the turn toward service also betrayed a genuine reorientation of railroad thinking away from the commodity-centered transport system envisioned by Morgan and toward a more diverse range of specialized services.

28 Kerr, *American Railroad Politics*, pp. 128–9 and 133.

29 Kerr, *American Railroad Politics*, esp. pp. 130–2.

30 "For the railroads", writes Kerr, "the term 'competition' did not refer to competition in rates, but only to competition in service." Kerr, *American Railroad Politics*, p. 156. On railroad proposals for reform, see Kerr, *American Railroad Politics*, pp. 150–6.

31 Kerr, *American Railroad Politics*, p. 155.

32 Kerr, whose careful study I otherwise greatly admire, dismisses the railroad appeal to service as a political ploy and characterizes their notion of a "competition in service" as a "pragmatic argument" designed to gain support of shippers. (He is at pains to minimize the importance of expressed shipper support for the railroads, discussed in the following paragraph.) Kerr sees a blatant "contradiction" on the part of railroads when they speak of competition in service while seeking to avoid competition in rates. While I acknowledge the difficulties of maintaining such a clear distinction in practice and while I recognize the elements of self-interest in the railroad proposal, I believe the railroad position reflected a genuine effort to reconcile their obligations as utilitarian common carriers with their desire to meet the growing demand for innovative services.

33 On shipper complaints about railroad service under wartime administration, see Kerr, *American Railroad Politics*, pp. 101–11 and 181–2.

34 Kerr, *American Railroad Politics*, pp. 187 and 193.

35 Kerr, *American Railroad Politics*, p. 193.

36 Kerr, *American Railroad Politics*, pp. 193–8.

37 William R. Childs, *Trucking and the Public Interest: The Emergence of Federal Regulation, 1914–1940* (Knoxville, 1985).

38 In addition to Childs, *Trucking and the Public Interest*, whose analysis I follow closely, this assessment of trucking regulation is derived from Galambos and Pratt, *Rise of the Corporate Commonwealth*, pp. 120–1, and Keller, *Regulating a New Economy*, pp. 66–76.

39 The standard source is Ernest Braun, *Revolution in Miniature: The History and Impact of Semiconductor Electronics* (New York, 1978). For additional information, see Kenneth Flamm, *Creating the Computer: Government, Industry, and High Technology* (Washington, DC, 1988); Richard C. Lewin, "The Semiconductor Industry", in Richard R. Nelson, ed., *Government and Technical Progress: A Cross-Industry Analysis* (New York, 1982), pp. 9–100; and David C. Mowery, "Innovation, Market Structure, and Government Policy in the American Semiconductor Electronics Industry: A Survey", *Research Policy* 12 (1983): 183–197. For an insightful introduction to the concept of natural trajectories and to the related idea of technological paradigms, see Giovanni Dosi, "Technological Paradigms and Technological Trajectories", *Research Policy* 11 (1982): 147–162. Borrowing from theories of scientific change, Dosi suggests that technology moves forward in waves, with a major breakthrough followed by a succession of modifications that

move naturally toward a readily perceptible end. He cites the semi-conductor industry as a prime example.

40 Gerald W. Brock, *The U.S. Computer Industry: A Study of Market Power* (Cambridge, Mass., 1975) and Flamm, *Creating the Computer* (Washington, DC, 1988).

41 Admittedly, those tasks initially did not seem all that diverse. Most involved complex calculations based on differential equations. Code-breaking represented a different application with important implications, but it was done in secret by the same sorts of people – mathematicians – using similar thought processes. It took a truly brilliant and prescient individual, such as Alan Turing, to recognize that those methods of reasoning could be used to resolve all sorts of problems. Even when applied to calculations, however, the computer had to be tailored or programmed to receive certain information, manipulate it in particular ways, and print out or store the results in a specific format. On Turing, see Andrew Hodges, *Alan Turing: The Enigma* (New York, 1983).

42 Emerson Pugh, *Memories that Shaped an Industry* (Cambridge, Mass., 1984).

43 See Richard R. Nelson, ed., *Government and Technical Progress: A Cross-Industry Analysis* (New York, 1982), esp. the essays by the editor, "Introduction" (pp. 1–9) and "Government Stimulus of Technological Progress: Lessons from American History" (pp. 451–82), and that by Barbara Goody Katz and Almarin Phillips, "The Computer Industry" (pp. 162–232). See also Bashe, *IBM's Early Computers*; Brock, *The U.S. Computer Industry*; Flamm, *Creating the Computer*; Lewin, "The Semiconductor Industry"; and Mowery, "Innovation, Market Structure, and Government Policy". On informed first users and other useful concepts for understanding government policy toward science and technology, see David C. Mowery and Nathan Rosenberg, *Technology and the Pursuit of Economic Growth* (Cambridge, 1989).

44 James W. Cortada, *Before the Computer: IBM, NCR, Burroughs, & Remington Rand & the Industry They Created* (Princeton, 1993); Arthur L. Norberg, "High-Technology Calculation in the Early 20th Century: Punched Card Machinery in Business and Government", *Technology and Culture* (1990); JoAnne Yates, "Co-evolution of Information-Processing"; Geoffrey Austrian, *Herman Hollerith: Forgotten Giant of Information Processing* (1982); Robert Sobel, *IBM: Colossus in Transition* (New York, 1981); and Steven W. Usselman, "IBM and Its Imitators: Organizational Capabilities and the Emergence of the International Computer Industry", *Business and Economic History*, Volume 22, No. 2 (Winter 1993): 1–35.

45 The analysis in this section closely follows that of Usselman, "IBM and Its Imitators", which in turn is derived from my monograph, "Creating System/360" (in progress). For a preliminary version, see Steven W. Usselman, "IBM: Making Waves in the Computer Business", a paper presented at the conference "Understanding Innovation", Johns Hopkins University, June 6–7, 1997. See also Emerson Pugh, et al., *IBM's 360 and Early 370 Systems* (Cambridge, Mass., 1991).

46 For an especially astute contemporary analysis from abroad, see Christopher Freeman, "Research and Development in Electronic Capital Goods", *National Institute Economic Review* 34 (November 1965): 40–97.

47 According to former IBM CEO Thomas J. Watson, Jr., antitrust concerns prevented IBM in 1949 from purchasing Eckert-Mauchly, the firm which first commercialized the electronic stored program computer. Antitrust concerns also influenced IBM's decision not to market solid state components in competition with Texas Instruments and other suppliers during the early 1960s. Usselman interview with Watson.

48 Sobel, *IBM: Colossus in Transition*.

49 On the parallels to broadcasting, see Steven W. Usselman, "Computer and Communications Technology", in Stanley Kutler, ed., *Encyclopedia of the United States in the Twentieth Century* (New York: Scribner's, 1996), pp. 799–829.

50 Usselman, "Creating System/360".

51 Flamm, *Creating the Computer*.

52 This analysis of the AT&T case and of the philosophy that underlay it closely follows that of Peter Temin, with Louis Galambos, *The Fall of the Bell System: A Study in Prices and Politics* (New York: Cambridge University Press, 1987).

53 For an excellent history and analysis of the minicomputer and microcomputer industries, see Richard N. Langlois, "External Economies and Economic Progress: The Case of the Microcomputer Industry", *Business History Review* 66 (1992): 1–50. This and the following three paragraphs owe much to this article.

54 The remainder of this paper is based on accounts widely available in the technical and business press.

55 In choosing to obtain its basic components under license from these two firms, IBM had at last fulfilled the prophecy of Mervin Kelly and seen its business pass into the hands of its suppliers. Why IBM chose this course remains something of a mystery. Some observers see the move as the product of the sort of rigidity that plagues large institutions. Typically, they cite comments by the head of the PC design team to the effect that he did not trust IBM's own semiconductor facility to make the processors a top priority. The PC group did not build its own semiconductor production line because IBM management did not want to duplicate facilities. Others have portrayed the move simply as a strategic blunder, in which managers facing intense time pressure failed to appreciate the longer term implications of their decision. Neither explanation, of course, fits the image of an organization skilled in striking the sorts of compromises necessary to keep it at the center of the industry. We would do well to remember, however, that IBM achieved far greater success with the PC than most analysts expected. Most believed a firm so tied to the business market could not respond to the demands of a mass consumer market. That IBM did so, even while continuing to thrive in its conventional arenas amid intense foreign competition, is in many ways quite a powerful testimony to its organizational flexibility. IBM pursued the licensing strategy, moreover, at a time when the Justice Department suit had stretched across a decade without resolution. By licensing the processor and the operating system, IBM assumed the sort of intermediary position antitrust regulators had often sanctioned, and which had proven so beneficial in the past.

56 Whether Sematech deserves any credit for the recovery of the American semiconductor industry remains a matter of some question. The decision not to renew its charter hardly suggests a ringing endorsement, though defenders stress that Sematech had performed a vital service and was simply no longer needed. Regardless of its effectiveness, however, the initiative certainly does nothing to diminish the perceived importance of flexible compromise to the computer industry. After all, it is precisely the ability to strike compromises that defenders claim for Sematech and that its detractors claim for the open market.

57 On railroading, see Steven W. Usselman, *Regulating Railroad Innovation: Business, Technology, and Politics in America, 1840–1920* (New York: Cambridge University Press, 2002) and Steven W. Usselman and Richard R. John, "Patent Politics: Intellectual Property, the Railroad Industry, and the Problem of Monopoly", *Journal of Policy History* 18,1(2006): 96–125; reprinted in Richard R. John, ed., *Ruling Passions: Political Economy in Nineteenth-Century America* (University Park, PA: Penn State University Press, 2006), pp. 96–125. Professor John's own work on telecommunications has elaborated on many of these themes. Cf. Richard R. John, *Network Nation: Inventing American Telecommunications* (Cambridge: Harvard University Press, 2010) and my review essay in *Business History Review* 85 (Autumn 2011): 603–615. For an update that also covers the twentieth century, see Steven W. Usselman, "Railroads", *The Oxford Encyclopedia of the History of Science, Medicine, and Technology* (New York:Oxford University Press, 2014), Hugh Richard Slotten, ed., Vol. 2, pp. 343–352. On computing, see Steven W. Usselman, "Computer and Communications Technology", in Stanley Kutler, ed., *The Encyclopedia of the United States in the Twentieth Century* (Scribner's, 1996), pp. 799–829, and Steven W, Usselman, "Fostering a Capacity for Compromise: Business, Government, and the Stages of Innovation in American Computing", *Annals of the History of Computing* Vol. 18, No. 2 (Summer 1996): 30–39.

58 For subsequent elaborations on the importance of antitrust to computing, see Steven W. Usselman, "Public Policies, Private Platforms: Antitrust and American Computing", in Richard C. Coopey, ed., *Information Technology Policy* (Oxford University Press, 2004), pp. 97–120; Steven W. Usselman, "Unbundling IBM: Antitrust and the Incentives to Innovation in American Computing", in Sally H.Clarke, Naomi R. Lamoreaux, and Steven W. Usselman, eds., *The Challenge of Remaining Innovative* (Palo Alto: Stanford University Press, 2009), pp. 249–279; and Steven W. Usselman and Barak D. Richman, "Elhague on Tying: Vindicated by History", *Tulsa Law Review* 49,3(Spring 2014): 689–711.

59 Chris Hughes, "It's Time to Break Up Facebook", *New York Times,* May 9, 2019, and Nick Clegg, "Breaking Up Facebook is Not the Answer", *New York Times*, May 11, 2019.

Chapter 2

Webs of productive association in American industrialization

Patterns of institution-formation and their limits, Philadelphia, 1880–1930

Philip Scranton

In recent years, historians of American industrialization have begun to turn away from national scale aggregate analyses and assumptions about the centrality of giant corporations to post-1880 economic development toward an emphasis on regional and local territorial complexes, multiple coevolving formats for production, and interfirm dynamics, within and across sectors, both informal and institutionalized. The decay of older industrial regions and fragility of the newer ones, the crisis restructuring of major companies, and the evaporation of what was expected to be an "American Century" have problematized the triumphalist, linear, and implicitly teleological accounts that dominated the industrialization literature for two generations after World War Two. One aspect of new research, sparked by the success of localized high-technology complexes, has concerned older industrial districts (spatial and sectoral concentrations of productively interconnected firms) and the institutions they fashioned to provide collective services and establish rules of business conduct, thus regulating competition through governance practice.[1]

This essay focuses upon the webs of affiliation in regional trade associations and similar business institutions which worked in numerous industrial districts to manage product and labor markets and influence politics during the early twentieth century. Drawing on approaches from economic geography and neo-institutionalism in economic sociology, it assesses the initiatives enterprisers undertook to engage shared dilemmas collectively, sketching the variety of associational forms and their limited achievements at the local/regional level in a major American industrial centre, Philadelphia. This effort represents something of a departure from the limited literature on business associations, most of which has centred on national-scale sectoral (American Iron and Steel Institute) or aggregate (National Association of Manufacturers) organizations. As research efforts increasingly focus on regional industrial agglomerations, however, it seems timely to probe the "associative impulse" at that scale, because as Howell Harris has observed, "employers associations are almost as neglected by . . . historians as are the kinds of firms that joined them".[2] Moreover, although Michael Porter argues that "the concepts and ideas" in his study of "why nations succeed in particular industries" may be "readily applied to political or geographic units smaller than a nation", and notes a variety of contemporary regional and urban concentrations in the United States, he does not pursue the question, while the limited attention given to trade associations in creating comparative advantages is, perhaps understandably in the present policy climate, confined to their role in framing strategies for transnational marketing.[3] To a degree, this study may provoke both reflection and research concerning the lacuna Harris identified and may "put some history behind" the relative marginalization of associational activity in Porter's framework. At a minimum, it will indicate that, at least in the US a century ago, manufacturers spent no little energy struggling together to address common problems, while competing for clients and capable staff, and that their success in this regard indeed in some measure derived from the characteristics of the "geographic units" they occupied.

In textiles and metalworking, Philadelphia's most prominent manufacturing sectors, trade groups attempted to mediate between firms and markets in order to avert "ruinous competition" for labor and orders or on terms of sale. Yet neither the Philadelphia Textile Manufacturers' Association (and other textile organizations) nor the Metal Manufacturers' Association of Philadelphia were particularly successful in this regard, unlike comparable local institutions in Cincinnati's machine tool industry or Grand Rapids' furniture trade. Other Philadelphia institutions, such as the Bourse, the Commercial Museum, and the Manufacturers' Club initiated cross-sectoral ventures in marketing and political lobbying. These too had at best modest effects, c. 1890–1940, when contrasted with other, comparable organizations (i.e. the Chicago Merchandise Mart or the Pennsylvania Manufacturers' Association).

To engage the disappointing results of regional business collectivism at Philadelphia, it will be helpful first to sketch the variety of industrial districts and the array of such institutions that dotted the American landscape in this era, in order to locate the Philadelphia experience within a larger, tentative framework. With this outline in hand, the local complement of organizations may be profiled and assessed against the efforts and experiences of similar contemporary assemblies, before proceeding to a few preliminary conclusions about Philadelphia's meso-level economic agencies. It must be noted at the outset that as industrially-centered and -spawned organizations faded during and after the Great Depression, a number of regional governmental or quasi-public institutions either commenced operations or grew in significance, addressing an imperfectly-overlapping set of issues germane to the business community's interests. This transition and any evaluation of this second cohort's efficacy lies beyond the compass of this paper, but is of considerable significance nonetheless.[4]

Conceptualizing industrial districts and trade organizations

As a new generation of literature concerning industrial districts accumulates,[5] it has become increasingly evident that these localized productive aggregations of firms linked by contract and custom in complex and flexible manufacturing networks were by no means homogeneous. Alfred Marshall's fabled Birmingham metal trades district has proven to be not a general model, but only one among a number of variations in form and process. Classically, industrial districts have drawn their special generative capacities from interdependencies within urban agglomerations that yielded "external economies", collective resources among trade specialists that facilitated rapid production of diversified goods more efficiently than could be expected at free-standing, integrated companies.[6] Yet a simple dichotomy between the giant self-sufficient (often mass production) corporation, like the Ford Motor Company in its River Rouge era, and a district of interconnected workshops, as at Birmingham or Solingen, remains too blunt an analytical tool. In between these extremes lay a number of formats that bear closer specification along dimensions of urban spatiality, autonomy and reciprocity, central pole *vs.* multilateral contracting, and issues of sectoral governance.[7]

Few great American corporations were as apparently autonomous as Ford (or in an earlier era, the Lowell textile corporations, with their machinery-building subsidiary, collectively-owned power company, and associated commission sales houses). More commonly, to take auto as an example, firms like Packard and Chrysler centralized design, assembly, finance, and marketing, while contracting out along two axes. Specifications for some parts were forwarded to metalworking firms scattered chiefly across second echelon midwestern cities. In tooling complex parts, for example, those involving stamping or templates, local tool and die firms were contacted for specialty work, whether the manufacturing was also outsourced or done in-house. Cumulatively, this latter practice built Detroit's renowned tool and die network as a vital adjunct to auto assemblers.[8] Being tied auxiliaries to a handful of major corporations, these clustered specialists little resembled an industrial district; they were instead virtuoso dependents with little other trade during seven months yearly of slack demand from automobile plants. Their distinction was their physical concentration near the industry's design and engineering hub, unlike thousands of other scattered industrial suppliers who serviced major manufacturers' staple and specialty needs through blizzards of crisscrossing orders and shipments.[9] One such purchaser was Philadelphia's Baldwin Locomotive Works, which made all its specialty metal goods inside, while contracting for standard parts (e.g., steel tires) in national markets, largely ignoring adjacent flexible metalworking firms.[10]

This variable mix of clientage and straight contracting can be termed *corporate standard* practice, in which a centre firm sets standards and specifications, and frames "make or buy" decisions based on assessments of company resources, capabilities and/or utilization levels. *Corporate localization* represents a slight variation from this motif. Here major enterprises responded routinely or episodically to their spatial embeddedness amid a host of specialist companies who could supply components, services, or added capacity through subcontracting or local purchasing of specialized equipment. Thus did Cramp, Sun Ship, and other Delaware Valley shipyards rely on dozens of area foundries, fabricators, machine shops, and toolmakers for vessel components, a logical step given delivery deadlines and bonuses or penalties for meeting them or failing to do so. So too did major Brass Valley non-ferrous producers (e.g., Scovill) call into service nearby Connecticut firms versed in the peculiar requirements of machining copper and brass, or farm out portions of rush contracts to them when existing production facilities were overloaded.[11] Propinquity, familiarity, and time-critical delivery could make the external economies of regional industrial districts valuable even to national-scale corporations. However, the extent to which such large firms facilitated the development of district capacities or were merely parasites on them, and the extent of reciprocity and trust between client and contractor cannot be gauged without further research.[12]

If we descend from the heights of the era's leading corporations to the realm of small and midsize firms (employing from dozens to multiple hundreds), industrial districts do not instantly materialize. Consider America's lumber mills, then found in the tens of thousands in every forested segment of the continent with staffs from a half-dozen to half a thousand; no agglomeration, no synergy, no districts. Consider bakeries and breweries, again ubiquitous, in sizable numbers at major urban centres, but lacking connectedness, interlocking specializations, and again not sparking districts.[13] Just as Alfred Chandler has noted the specificity of trades prone to the technical and organizational dynamics that yielded oligopolistic "modern business enterprise[s]",[14] so too in the fashioning of industrial districts, a host of non-trivial trades were non-starters: bricks and stone, nails and fasteners, most staple textiles and paper-making, as well as newspapers, and the sectors mentioned above. These were predominantly resource-site dependent processors of materials, manufacturers of simple staples, or local market purveyors of perishable goods. Though their histories deserve attention, it cannot be afforded them here.

Where then in the universe of manufacturing sectors and spaces might one expect to find industrial districts, and in what variety? From my earlier work,[15] it seems that they should be most likely to develop in cities and city-regions featuring industries generating final consumer and producer goods characterized by product diversity, batch rather than bulk or mass outputs, persistent market uncertainties, a shifting mix of mid-size and smaller companies, and a significant presence in their national trades. These configurations of opportunity and hazard press individual firms toward webs of association at the local–regional level, toward collaborative institutions that identify producers' shared concerns and prosecute programmes and practices that address them. This is to say that an element of institution-building and initiatives toward trade governance signal a maturing industrial district, without assuring that the goals imagined will prove achievable given the district's sectoral and conjunctural context.[16]

These boundaries then identify industrial districts as being theoretically feasible in at least the following sectors: machinery and machine tools, heavy transportation equipment, specialty metalworking, fashion textiles and apparel, furniture, publishing and printing (excluding newspapers), styled consumer goods (leather work, jewelry and silverware, shoes, etc.), and technical/scientific instrumentation.[17] Excluded are dozens of "niche" sectors, like billiard tables or office supplies, which were either too tiny to generate agglomeration advantages or too diffuse to make production location a significant magnet for spatial concentration (leading to their dominance by wholesalers who gathered for resale the products of widely-dispersed specialists). Mapping these sectors and these expectations against the practice of urban batch specialists in early twentieth-century America yields a diverse array of plausible industrial districts, some of which featured what can be called the practice of *localized mutuality*, effective collaboration to varying degrees, and others that operated in a context of *localized opportunism*, blunting or constraining efforts at sustaining trade solidarity.[18]

These urban-focused industrial districts can be linked conceptually to their cities of origin along four channels of differentiation: monoculture, enclaves, parallelism, and interaction. Monocultures are in a sense an industrial district analogy to the well known company towns of extra-urban northern industrialization and much of southern textile development.[19] Rather than being dominated (and at times planned) by a single, huge enterprise (Amoskeag in Manchester, NH; Dayton's National Cash Register, or the Pullman complex at Chicago's southern edge), monoculture districts arose chiefly in secondary cities that, *c.* 1850–1890, became hubs for entrepreneurship in a specific sector whose multiplying enterprises shaped a distinctive industrial character. Of course other, often local-market-oriented trades developed at such sites, but in Massachusetts, Lynn and Haverill were noted for shoes, Holyoke for fine papers. In Connecticut, Meriden stood at the centre of the silverplate trades and New Britain meant hardware and tools. New Jersey's Paterson was "Silk City", whereas Grand Rapids, MI, and Jamestown, NY, were furniture centres, and in the new century, Reading, PA, anchored a knitting district. In each case, multiple final goods producers fashioned thick webs of association with auxiliary firms that made castings, drafted designs, contracted for carving ornamentation, dyed yarns and piece goods, created intermediate materials and components, or built and repaired special machinery. Monoculture districts drew migrating or immigrant workers magnetically, and at each site manufacturers clubbed together in organizations to advance their shared interests.

By contrast, enclaves represented clusters of specialists in cities more or less dominated by great bulk or mass production sectors. Overshadowed by giant meatpackers and steel magnates, Chicago's furniture stylists came quietly to dominate the upholstered parlour goods trade by the 1920s.[20] Scores of fine pressed and blown glass firms operated skillfully in the Pittsburgh district, even as steel's Carnegie, Frick, Jones, and Laughlin, and routinized window glass operations (which ultimately became Pittsburgh Plate Glass) claimed centre stage.[21] As Cincinnati's reputation was being built on making cheap work clothes, processing hogs into cured meats, and rendering by-products into Procter & Gamble's early soaps, the rudiments of the nation's most creative machine tool district were being articulated.[22] While twentieth-century Los Angeles was becoming a west coast locus for mass production branch plants, incoming specialists erected fashion-oriented furniture and apparel complexes.[23] Enclaves thus are unsuspected, often nearly-invisible, flexible complexes lodged in the interstices of city regions whose principal developmental trajectories have been led by corporate bulk processing initiatives. Consistently, however, their strategic appropriation of sectoral opportunities nationally proved more critical to success than linkages with leading regional bulk and mass output trades.

The two final categories that link sector and place speak to patterns evident in larger northeastern cities where batch and specialty manufacturing was more the norm than the exception. Parallelism refers to diversified cities wherein several industrial districts coexisted without significant generative contacts among them, while interaction signals the presence of just such productive connectivity. On the first count, Providence, Rhode Island supported an extensive jewelry and silverware sector, a substantial concentration of styled textile companies in worsteds and lace, and an important metalworking complex led by Brown and Sharpe and Corliss Engine. Though the latter supplied some tools and prime movers to jewelers and weaving mills, their main market orientations were national, not regional. On Manhattan, similarly, the nation's greatest concentration of apparel specialists cohabited with, but rarely encountered New York's high-end jewelry and diamond trades and its awesome array of printers and publishers.[24] By contrast, Worcester, Massachusetts' antebellum prowess in fashioning textile machinery and machine tools gradually spawned clusters of enterprises making carpets, thread, and woollens, others devoted to small tools, weapons, agricultural implements and wire, and a host of allied machinery builders for shoes, metal shaping and grinding, paper and stationery, power transmission, and the associated industrial (or "mill") supplies.[25] Comparable patterns obtained in and around Newark, NJ, whose tool builders, ferrous and non-ferrous metal fabricators, and other specialists laid the groundwork both for Edison's "invention factory" and the region's subsequent electrical trades. Philadelphia, perhaps more than any other diversified urban manufacturing site, sported complexes of interaction among divisions of its extensive metals and fashion textile sectors, and through the machinery nexus, between these two giant specialty industries. The outcome was both the articulation of product and technical novelty and the creation of an extraordinary array of collective institutions.

This suggestion of diversity in production localizations and industrial districts is complemented by the wide variation of trade institutions in early twentieth-century American manufacturing, the third aspect of this preliminary framework. Such organizations operated in at least ten formats, five local-regional, one bridge category, and four national. The local-regional associations can be categorized as: subsectoral, sectoral, cross-sectoral, marketing, and professional groups. The bridge class includes localized divisions of national institutions, some of which actually were the bases on which the latter were erected. National-scale institutions were chiefly sectoral, cross-sectoral, market-organizing, and professional. Examples of this welter of variations are obviously necessary, and here will be drawn chiefly from the Philadelphia context.

1   Area sub-sectoral: In any broad, regionally-concentrated indus-
    trial sector with a sizable diversity of specialist component trades,
    modest-scale enterprises will have incentives to organize collec-
    tives that may help them frame common policies toward suppliers,
    contractual clients, labour, tariff politics, shifts in technology, extra-
    regional competitors, etc. In Philadelphia textiles, such issues were
    embraced by the Carpet Yarn Spinners Association, the Full Fash-
    ioned Hosiery Manufacturers' Association, the Master Dyers Asso-
    ciation, and a number of other groups in upholstery, carpets, worsted
    spinning, etc. Few of these had permanent staff or office quarters,
    meeting instead episodically in hotels or club rooms to deal with
    challenges or crises that labour organizing or a threatened tariff revi-
    sion offered. Most maintained contact with or formal membership in
    sector-wide associations.

2   Area sectoral: These were industry-specific, but regional, "peak"
    associations, making an effort to adjust the tensions and snags
    among sub-sectoral groups and/or present a common front to
    labour, railways, the state, or non-local trade rivals (and potential
    collaborators). In the Quaker City, one can readily identify the Metal
    Manufacturers' Association of Philadelphia, the Philadelphia Tex-
    tile Manufacturers' Association, the Boot and Shoe Association of
    Philadelphia, and elsewhere, the Grand Rapids Furniture Manufac-
    turers' Association, and the larger-scope, separate New England
    Cotton and Woolen Manufacturers' Associations. Here permanent
    staff and operations were common, and officers were expected to
    perform far more than ceremonial duties. Member firms could ben-
    efit from labour bureaus, collective purchasing or warehousing, and/
    or regular updates on technical or political problems, but might be
    expected to provide survey data for policy initiatives or to finance
    ventures into technical education or factory law lobbying.[26]

3   Area cross-sectoral: Integrative associations and clubs provided ven-
    ues for enterprise owners and top managers to share their perspectives

on the broadest set of issues that might impact on district or regional economic prospects, i.e., tariffs, immigration, federal/state/local tax policies, state and national party politics, insurance and liability (and in general, the law from patents to injunctions), among other matters. In Philadelphia such organizations included the Cosmopolitan Club, drawing on the thickly-industrialized Northeast districts, the generalist and powerful Manufacturers' Club, the inclusive Board of Trade and Chamber of Commerce (which included bankers, retailers/wholesalers, and railroads), and the Union League (where key industrialists mingled with Philadelphia's Republican elite in law, real estate, and finance). Elsewhere, such areal integrators might be found at the Employers' Association of Detroit, Cincinnati's Queen City Club, or state-level manufacturers' associations in Pennsylvania, Connecticut, et al. Their local-regional political impact was often determinant, their presence in congressional hearings rooms to be expected, as was their provision of salient services, including group fire, liability, and workmen's compensation insurance, valued by business members.[27] Many maintained sumptuous quarters that expressed an image of productive entitlement while offering spaces for sectoral and sub-sectoral association conferences as well as whist tournaments, private rooms for deal-making dinners, and reception halls for honouring visiting dignitaries and Presidential candidates.[28]

4   Area marketing: It was relatively straightforward for regionally-concentrated enterprises to league together to reach some measure of concurrence with local trade colleagues or contest or cajole known "others",[29] but marketing necessitated reaching out to a far more ambiguous and virtual (rather than co-present) clientele. For the Chandlerist, oligopolizing corporation, integrating forward into marketing did have its hazards, but resources interior to the firm could be brought to bear on pushing brand names through advertising, spreading service outlets spatially, or capturing distributional channels through contract or acquisition.[30] For modest sized, national-market-oriented, final goods firms enmeshed in regional industrial complexes, these options were either prohibitively expensive or simply implausible. Thus, the emergence of collective sales institutions was a sensible tactical step for those who sought to draw unknown buyers to a centre of concentrated supply for specialty products.[31]

Leading the way in Philadelphia were the Bourse and the Commercial Museum, both products of the 1890s. The Bourse, an elegant, centrally-located edifice, housed selling and demonstration spaces for hundreds of the city's more prominent manufacturing firms, largely drawn from the textile, machinery and metal trades, whose production sites were scattered across the northeast/northwest Philadelphia manufacturing belt several miles distant.[32] By the 1930s, the Bourse had 2500 members and 500 resident tenants, including the offices of the Board of Trade, the Commercial Exchange, the Maritime Exchange, the Association of Manufacturers' Representatives, and other organizations united under the slogan: "buy, sell, ship via Philadelphia". Though each focused on its special concerns, "practically all of them [were] allied in various joint movements having for their purpose the commercial welfare of the city".[33]

Though ostensibly a national institution, the Commercial Museum was designed to exhibit Philadelphia products that might have export potential as well as samples of usable, foreign-originating raw materials. It regularly held export fairs and provided firms with leads or contacts to importing agencies in Europe, South America, and Asia, plus credit reports, and details on foreign trade customs and regulations. Closely allied with the Manufacturers' Club, it occupied a spacious marble building adjacent to the University of Pennsylvania campus at the central city's western edge.[34] Other comparable market organizing institutions included the Builders' Exchange, the Drug Exchange, and the Ocean Traffic Bureau. Though Philadelphia may have been extremely profuse in supporting such collectives, their counterparts may be found in the Grand Rapids Furniture Market Exposition Association and copycat furnishing-sales institutions created at Jamestown, NY, Chicago, and High Point, NC, in the wake of Grand Rapids' success, and for comprehensive consumer goods, the Chicago Merchandise Mart.[35]

5   Area professional: As the salience of situated shop knowledge was gradually displaced both by the formalized scientism of engineering principles and by networking among skilled workers and foremen (promoted by exchanges in the expanding industrial journal literature), local cross-firm and intersectoral collectives of critical personnel took shape in the decades surrounding the turn of the century. In their associations and societies, such as Philadelphia's Engineers' Club, individuals could extract themselves from the daily press of production imperatives for monthly discussions that bore on key challenges they confronted in their work, supplemented by full measures of dining and conviviality. The most ambitious and

well-funded of these regional professional groups, like Philadelphia's engineers, occupied permanent facilities, published proceedings of their sessions, and hosted annual gatherings of trade-related professional groups. Similar clusters (and often journals) appeared among engineers in St Louis, Pittsburgh, etc., as did associations of textile overseers in central New England and of electroplaters in the Newark/New York district, and elsewhere.[36]

6   Bridges – areal divisions of national associations: Near the turn of the twentieth century, predominantly in the metal industries, but also in some consumer goods sectors, federations of regional trade associations gathered momentum in considerable measure as a response to locally-focused, but nationally-significant organizing efforts by skilled labourers. Hence the Philadelphia sections of the National Metal Trades Association and the National Founders Association were active elements in a set of larger contests that involved branches at Worcester, Providence, Cleveland, Cincinnati, Chicago, et al. Though well-staffed national organizations undertook to guide collective policies, regional branches exercised considerable autonomy that often vexed their ostensible leadership cadres.[37] In addition, some locally-originating groupings, as in Cincinnati machine tools, rapidly developed into national-scale associations, in this case the National Machine Tool Builders' Association, which also attempted to coordinate policies among toolmakers clustered at a dozen or so key locales in the United States. Branch operations' membership frequently overlapped with sectoral or cross-sectoral regional associations, for example, the Philadelphia MMA, creating ample spaces for inter-organizational tensions and rivalries.[38] The "search for order" in early twentieth-century America regularly involved clashes between differing visions of order at different scales of action and conceptualization, with unsurprisingly unpredictable outcomes.

7   National sectoral: These institutions have garnered the lion's share of attention in efforts to track business collectivism in America. When, in the 1920s and 1930s, business association activities were a matter of public policy and scholarly concern, national industry organizations drew the fire of the Federal Trade Commission and the courts, along with the more solicitous scrutiny of economists and political scientists.[39] They figured largely in federal actions against price-fixing and other efforts to deflect "fair" competition. At the same time the Hoover Commerce Department of the 1920s regarded them as a potential means for rationalizing business practice through promotion

of standard cost-accounting procedures, elimination of wasteful product varieties, and elaboration of voluntary measures to promote efficiency, consumer education, export marketing, and allied goals of business neo-progressivism, and later were the keystone of the ill-fated National Recovery Association's code authorities.[40] In their hundreds they covered the entire manufacturing spectrum from raw lumber to fine hosiery, from the grossest bulk production to the most specialized outputs. Though detailed studies of such organizations are rare,[41] many appear to have largely been lobbying fronts and anti-union coalitions, devoted to preserving tariff advantages and fighting efforts at liberalizing labour laws at state and federal levels. Some, like machine tools' NMBTA, pressed for solidarity against price-cutting in volatile-demand trades, whereas the American Iron and Steel Institute pushed for tariff protection and the development of standards and materials research. Others, such as the National Wool Manufacturers' Association, combined tariff defence with publications gauging the character of international competition and materials' supply dilemmas, all the while celebrating their sector's role in building American industrial prowess. There is no adequate analysis of this mass of collectivities, because they would first have to be judged significant (and "significant to what?" specified) before their diversity could be engaged, conceptualized, and addressed critically.[42]

8   National cross-sectoral: Three "peak" organizations dominated this class, c. 1900–1940. The National Association of Manufacturers, whose first two presidents were Philadelphia "textile men" and Manufacturers' Club leaders, principally represented the varied interests of firms in competitive sectors. Its spokesmen fought government and organized labour "interference" in business matters, while promoting standard cost accounting and export opportunities. The National Industrial Conference Board marshalled the forces of big business in oligopolistic sectors seeking to manage regulation and markets and tame the wild swings of the business cycle. Its research publications and high profile conferences gave it both visibility and a rather more progressive tone than the NAM. Finally, the U.S. Chamber of Commerce was a federation of inclusive local and state associations that attempted to harmonize the interests of retailers, producers, and service sector firms, most notably at the small business end of the scale spectrum.[43]

9   National marketing: Given the strictures of American anti-trust law on market-related collusion, these market-making institutions took two forms. One was the independent real estate development

company, often subscribed to by manufacturers, that erected Bourse-like structures to concentrate sectorally specific sales offices, as at the Textile Building and the Garment Center in Manhattan, or Chicago's American Furniture Mart, which commenced as a regional selling center and was succeeded in 1930 by a massive consumer durables warehousing and distribution complex, the Merchandise Mart. These were confined chiefly to consumer goods sectors with thousands of potential retail buyers, and aimed at achieving a critical mass of producers and wholesalers sufficient to draw them magnetically to a single site. The other form involved corporations that could undertake legal interfirm collaboration for export purposes only, a practice legitimized under the Webb-Pomerene Act of 1918. These surfaced chiefly in raw materials sectors and were of relatively minor importance into the 1930s.[44]

10   National professional: The best-known professional organizations in industrial circles are those among engineers, first the American Society of Mechanical Engineers in the 1880s, followed by groupings of electrical, chemical, and other specialists. Their annual conventions, published proceedings, branch activities, and special project task forces consistently engaged problems of technological innovation, industrial "best practice", education and training, and increasingly, safety, testing, and standardization. In addition, associations of industrial managers sprouted by the turn of the century, ranging from the sectorally-focused wool and worsted spinning overseers to more generalist organizations of accountants and personnel officers. The umbrella Associated Engineering Societies sponsored the much-debated *Waste in Industry* study after World War One but faded away in the 1920s. By contrast, the American Management Association grew steadily in influence, publishing reams of advisory pamphlets, pressing for professionalized managerial education, and holding scores of conferences and seminars.

Even this extensive roster does not exhaust the full range of cross-firm institutions, for it omits collectively initiated banks, schools, and research institutes along with private-public partnerships.[45] How best may one think critically and imaginatively about this variegated mass? As the "new institutionalism" has made headway in economic and public policy research,[46] it is perhaps sensible to attempt to locate theoretical perspectives that bear on this profusion and may help explicate both the differentiation and differential effectiveness of manufacturing collectivities in the Philadelphia region.

Institutional theory, governance and trust

The revival of institutional theory stems doubly from dissatisfaction with the reductionist and ahistorical insufficiencies of neo-classical economics on one hand, and the excessive formalism and hyperrationality of organizational analysis on the other.[47] Among other things, "new institutionalists" are especially concerned with contextual-environmental diversities, contingency, conflict, the historical patterning of institutional change, and from Anthony Giddens, "the increased 'structuration' of interorganizational relations".[48] To date, the bulk of its practitioners' research has focused on governments and nonprofits, but Walter Powell has recently argued that "more attention [must] be directed toward such core sectors of the economy as manufacturing and finance", adding that "American society generates many levels and types of organizations, with overlapping responsibilities, organizational interpenetration, and systems of partial and fragmented governance".[49] The preceding roster of associational forms suggests that what Powell and others regard as core elements of underdetermination in the U.S. political apparatus may well have been mirrored among its economic institutions.[50] The attenuation and eclipse of local-regional trade groups, which seems to have occurred in the generation after 1930, may be congruent with new institutionalist theorists' arguments concerning interactive state-economy dynamics pressing toward an incomplete (and perhaps inefficient) rationalization and centralization of institutional capacities at the national level. In any event, the potential for productive empirical-theoretical exchanges between scholars of industrial organization and restructuring and this cadre of "open system" analysts seems substantial.[51]

Powell's mention of "fragmented governance" brings into play issues critical to the functioning of industrial districts and regional manufacturing complexes: the means through which relational rules and routines for business practice are established and sustained. For some time following Shonfield's seminal study,[52] governance was presumed to be unitary within but variable across nation states and to concern chiefly business-state contests and negotiations about the rules of economic play. Subsequent critics pointed out, however, the presence of significant intra-national governance variance across industrial sectors and argued that "the success of industrial strategies may depend more on sectoral governance structures than on national ones".[53] Kitschelt and others now have undertaken to differentiate sectors according to their technological endowments and trajectories (and by implication, their market contexts), in order to elaborate an array of situationally-optimal governance patterns, drawing on Perrow's notions of tight *vs.* loose coupling and linear *vs.* complex technical systems.[54] Broadly, these considerations suggest four patterns of governance:

1   Centralization/hierarchy, derived from tight coupling and linearity – for example, basic metals, chemicals
2   Decentralized lateral coordination networks, flowing from loose coupling and complex interactions – for example, specialty production, software, biotechnology)
3   Market ordering and minimalist coordination, in settings of loose coupling and linearity – for example, staple consumer goods, coal
4   Contradictory/failure-prone coordination, in sectors where tight coupling and complex interaction demand both centralization to prevent rapid system spread of errors and decentralization "to avoid information overload at the top" – for example, nineteenth-century railroads, nuclear power, aerospace[55]

Though this framework is provocative along a number of avenues, here its second category usefully brackets the relational imperatives of industrial districts and their associated collective organizations in areas like Philadelphia. Consistent with Scott's observation that "organizations will tend to map the complexity of environmental elements into their own structures", Philadelphia's networked district firms created a melange of local and regional institutions that overlapped functions, displayed elements of hierarchy without comparable mechanisms of control, and evolved "through an adaptive, unplanned, historical process".[56] Governance, like production, was decentralized, reactive, and laterally configured, reliant as much on voluntarism and social expectations of right behavior as on services or sanctions.[57] This necessity leads toward a focus on trust.

Both centralized and hierarchical governance systems and those organized around market ordering represent low-trust environments, in that either legitimized authority or price competition and contract law establishes rules and routines. By contrast, the decentralized lateral governance characteristic of industrial districts calls for a high-trust context: individuals must have confidence that their colleagues will behave neither as opportunists nor as "free riders" in order for productive fluidity/flexibility and social reciprocity/solidarity to be sustained.[58] Formally, trust relations underlie the efforts of associated firms to provide collective services. They centre on expectations that trade colleagues will adhere to accepted norms of competition and collaboration, including, for example, maintenance of quality and timeliness, willingness to assist in problem-solving or to share technical information, and refraining from wage rivalry, worker poaching, and often, dealings with unions.[59] In this era's industrial districts, frequent face-to-face (rather than distantiated) dealings, shared ethnic/religious backgrounds, and common business and political values all contributed to the construction of reciprocity and high-trust relations that made oral commitments binding and crafted a basis for private rather than litigated dispute settlements.

In essence, trust relations represent behavioural outcomes based on a conception of collective interest, yet in research thus far, questions concerning the boundaries of that collective, how they are defined, extended, and maintained, and concerning the connection between mechanisms of trust-based governance and their spatial and socio-political contexts, have been underexplored. On the last issue, Lorenz is helpful, however, suggesting that informal ("decentralized") means of reinforcing norms (direct expressions of approval or disapproval, threats of terminating reciprocity) "work best in small and stable communities", whereas institutionalized ("centralized") means "reflect the relative openness of nineteenth- and twentieth-century industrial districts to outsiders" who may have "limited economic dependence on insiders and . . . lack [their] common values".[60] Greater attention has been paid to breakdowns, which case studies suggest derive from either recession/crisis-induced violations of reciprocity norms or rising economic opportunities that "encourag[ed some] producers to break their established ties with the community".[61]

European examples suggest the districts that best moderated these disruptive forces were those which erected institutions whose power to sanction self-interested opportunism, educate incomers to area norms, and encourage innovations in technology and marketing was legitimated by the state.[62] With these conceptual tools in hand, we may turn to twentieth century Philadelphia.

Philadelphia and the challenges of business collectivism

Brief profiles of and commentaries on the initiatives and inadequacies of three Philadelphia trade institutions will serve here to illustrate both the determination and frustrations of manufacturers associated in efforts at industrial governance, c. 1900–1930. One each has been drawn from sub-sectoral, sectoral, and cross-sectoral organizations, respectively the Full-Fashioned Hosiery Manufacturers' Association (FHMA), the Metal

Manufacturers' Association (MMA), and the Manufacturers' Club. With these sketches in hand, the Philadelphians will be contrasted with rather more successful trade bodies, furniture manufacturers in Grand Rapids, Michigan and machine tool companies at Cincinnati, providing a basis for an attempt to account for the former's far less robust achievements.

Thirteen makers of seamed, contoured silk and cotton women's hosiery formed the FHMA during World War One. The trade was new to Philadelphia and the United States, being the product of technical transfer of German-designed machinery (*c.* 1900) and the physical relocation of key innovators who formed the Textile Machine Works at Reading, PA, sixty miles northwest of the metropolis. This sectoral subdivision had grown dramatically before the war at the nation's most developed knitting centre, but its technological complexities mandated employment of scarce, highly-skilled workers who rapidly organized a hosiery union that soon regulated apprenticeship training and demanded rate increases in tandem with wartime inflation. The FHMA thus was reactive and focused on gaining control over labour relations, job tasking, and training, all in a highly volatile market and technical context.[63]

The Association met serious difficulties from the outset. The newest and smallest companies (some started by experienced workers) and at least one larger firm refused to join; though in the first confrontation with labour (1919), they shrewdly affirmed they would accept any settlement the FMHA secured, then ran full bore while association members stood idle during the ensuing strike. The FMHA led a coalition of other subsectoral organizations in offering a collaborative "Textile Council" to generate harmony, install profit-sharing, and combat "bolshevism". This transparent ploy was instantly rejected by unionists and mocked by federal labour mediators as a delusory "open road to an industrial millennium . . . although the workers have not been invited to participate in working out the rules and regulations".[64] Union solidarity and swelling post-war demand for consumer fashions defeated the FHMA in 1919.

Two years later, amid a sudden and sharp depression, the association took the offensive, demanding labour process changes that would assign skilled knitters two machines, radically increase the numbers of apprentices, and lower piece rates by 15%. It was again stalemated. Though member firms and crisis allies controlled five-sixths of Philadelphia full-fashioned jobs, two sizable Reading firms (one started by the market-alert TMW owners) prospered hugely, "largely as a result of labor troubles in Philadelphia". The allies soon caved in, but fourteen core association members held fast until a compromise terminated the ten-month walkout.[65]

The dramatic surge in demand for full-fashioned silk hose throughout the 1920s muted labour battling, and the FMHA receded in significance, becoming a grumble-and-gripe society for anti-union employers. When the rise of southern hosiery rivals (combined with regional expansions) yielded excess capacity, falling prices, market advantages to hosiery purchasers, and fresh union organizing campaigns (trade problems appearing just before and aggravated by the Great Depression), the core FMHA firms undertook to organize nationally. Again they failed, for Dixie companies saw no reason to ally themselves with the bedevilled Yankees. Unionists' efforts to control ruinous competition through standardizing wage costs at least regionally, and potentially nationwide, were also completely balked.[66] What went wrong?

Structurally, given the preceding theoretical literature, the co-located constituencies for the FMHA were well short of the necessary prerequisites to frame a vital governance institution. There was no preceding knitting trades association from which it might have sprouted as a new subdivision. Given massively-expanding sales in the 1920s, sectoral operations, despite their initial regional concentration, were readily replicated at first near machinery suppliers and later in the southern states' cheaper labour districts. Additionally, local trade insiders, notably veteran workers, busily created new firms and resisted collective commitments that might constrain their efforts at seizing market shares.

Operationally, the association could not draw on a compelling logic of collective needs and values, other than hostility to labour unions, a deficiency which could be situationally parlayed into short term tactical advantages for non-complying firms. It made no attempt to conjure up a training institute, a collective marketing center, or a testing and technology assessment function. Product diversity and rapidly-changing technical conditions made efforts at price-control or common selling and discount policies a chimera. Early attempts to lead a common front among collateral subsectoral associations foundered on the rocks of disparate group interests, and the FHMA developed no overarching analysis that might have provided a foundation for a wider sectoral appreciation of collective needs. Further, as neither import competition nor substitution threats from rival fibers and fabrics were salient, key lines of potential associational solidarity proved irrelevant.[67] When the market power of major buyers grew in an environment of overcapacity and increasing standardization of basic hosiery styles, this trade institution could provide no means beyond ineffectual moral suasion to prevent special dealing, price and terms concessions, and a wider "demoralization" of the trade. It failed fully and completely.[68]

The Metal Manufacturers' Association charted a more satisfactory course, surmounting substantial obstacles in reaching its aims. The metal trades were Philadelphia's second largest industry at the turn of the century, employing over 30,000 workers, nearly half of whom toiled at great enterprises: Baldwin Locomotive, Cramp's shipyards, Midvale Steel, Disston Saw, and Brill's streetcar manufactory. A large number of firms, but a small percentage of the workforce, operated at the other extremity of scale as tiny machine shops, independent pattern-makers and the like. The MMA, whose 1903 founding was a reaction to organizing drives of the national molders' and machinists' unions (c. 1898–1904), was ignored by the "big five" and itself bypassed the city's tiny shops. Its constituency was chiefly midsize firms (50–500 employees) in all divisions of the local metal trades. Although it drew only 100 or so member firms (c. 10% of area enterprises), the MMA "covered" about one-third of the metalworking labour force, and well over half of that in machine tools and machine shops.[69]

From the outset, the organization focused on labour relations. It rarely lobbied and had no research or marketing arm. Statewide generalist and national sectoral associations (PMA, NMTA, NFA) handled politics, and most members dealt directly with clients and tracked new technical activity through dinner conferences of the Engineers' Club or section meetings at the Manufacturers' Club.[70] As Harris noted, "the MMA existed, first and foremost, for strikebreaking", and unlike textile groups, could boast that it never lost a strike "for any member with the guts to fight to the finish".[71] Its turn of the century labour battles drew an initial membership complement, but retaining firms after the crisis ebbed was a challenge that MMA leaders met by crafting an institution to manage the employment market on a day-to-day basis, the Labor Bureau. The five giants needed no such mediating collaborative; their scale enabled them to internalize ordinary recruitment and hire commercial strikebreaking agencies when required. But for midsize firms critically dependent on skilled labour, such an operation was especially valuable, particularly because batch and custom work came in spurts and forces had to be expanded rapidly with reliable, competent men. Providing this service, the Labor Bureau anchored companies to the MMA for decades; and given firm-level peaks and valleys in orders and hence employment, it likewise provided "next job" referrals for thousands of laid-off workers.[72]

The Labor Bureau allowed metalworking plants to bypass union business agents, newspaper advertising, and foremen's friends, and ended up poaching workers from others' shops along with the accompanying wage-bidding. Unlike NMTA bureaus on which it was modelled the

MMA's labour exchange was not flatly anti-unionist,[73] but welcomed workers whether affiliated or independent, a position consistent with the varied policies of member companies. Harris summarized its advantages: "a centrally-located office for one stop job shopping for skilled metal tradesmen; a courteous reception; no fees to either side; no obligation – the bureau only recommended a man to a firm, the foreman, superintendent or proprietor did the actual hiring". Thus, the MMA was a pure "open shop" advocate, avoiding blacklists yet expelling member firms that entered into formal contracts with unions. Moreover, as workers shifted jobs, their Bureau employment records "turned into a sort of certificate of competence, or at least proof of experience", reducing the number of bad hires firms endured and speeding the acceptance of the temporarily unemployed at new posts.[74] Voluntarism reigned over all transactions; the Bureau was a service rather than an obligation. Hence firms and workers could also use other tracks to match jobs and skills, and each was free, as noted above, to decline the place or man recommended.[75]

After World War One, the MMA expanded its labour provision roles, creating a set of "cooperative training programs for foremen and machinists' apprentices", as a means to resupply the skills pool now that veteran immigrant workers were no longer readily available. It collaborated with university research projects on personnel practices, and drew into its membership several of the region's relatively new capital-goods plants (GE and Westinghouse). Yet almost every effort made to step beyond the confines of labour issues failed. Members were not galvanized by appeals to "give one another preference in their business dealings", rejected efforts to install standard cost accounting practices, and showed no interest in transforming the MMA into a "joint research and development agency" for its constituents. Their engagement with the association was instrumental and tightly constrained by its initial mission. Its services built a measure of trust in its competences, but members' indifference to larger projects showed their "strictly limited commitment to the virtues of collectivism".[76] Though it could regularize the labour market's dual-sided search process, and to a degree promote programs that would assist skills reproduction, the MMA had neither the warrant nor the wherewithal to extend the scope of its functions. As the regional metal trades' decline commenced during the Great Depression and resumed after the war surge, the organization had neither moral nor material capacities to address mounting problems and faded into insignificance.[77]

Alone among this trio, the Manufacturers' Club lives yet, but only in the form of a luxuriant golf course and country club just outside

Philadelphia's city boundaries. Its rise and recalibration into a center for monied leisure inscribes the trajectory of regional "peak" institutions before 1940. The club was formed in 1887 as a means to extend the successful collaboration of textile manufacturers who had allied in opposition to the Knights of Labor during the 1886 strike wave. Though its initial base was in the fabric trades, several of its early leaders were major figures in other sectors as well.[78] Membership grew from 147 after the organizing meeting to 500 within several months, and over a thousand by 1895. Its anti-union origins were quickly left behind, and clubmen turned to acting on their "earnest desire . . . to purchase of each other", to "mold[ing] the conditions of trade . . . in their favor", and to influencing governments on behalf of manufacturing generally and with regard to particular sectors well-established in Philadelphia. The first aim was met by providing private rooms of several sizes for business dinners and by publishing a comprehensive members' list organized by "business classification". The second yielded the formation of "sections" through which "classes of manufacturers" could treat with shippers, wholesalers, etc. on issues of shared concern and through creating the Bourse, which was "born in the Manufacturers' Club". The third proceeded by way of resolutions and memorials voted by the whole membership or by sections and conveyed by "special committees" to city hall and state and federal capitals for consideration. By 1895, fewer than a quarter of the membership flowed from textile interests, and the club had made good on its intention to inaugurate "an organization embracing all the different manufacturing industries".[79]

The club's journal, aptly dubbed *The Manufacturer*, appeared late in 1887 and soon doubled its size and frequency, becoming a weekly two years later. Reliably Republican and protectionist, the clubmen and their journal cut large figures both regionally and nationally. Their efforts blocked local ordinances that would have increased manufacturing costs, supported infrastructure improvements (elevated rail transit) that widened labour sheds, and forced revisions of Pennsylvania workmen's compensation and factory inspection laws (in tandem with the PMA), though members remained deeply divided on bimetallism, unions, and railroad rate regulation. Locally, the club sponsored debates among members on political topics (the Free Speech Club) and public lectures at a large nearby auditorium, feted leading GOP politicians, opened its rooms to trade societies, and printed weekly rosters giving the night's members would be "in-house" to receive friends and business associates, presumably for drinks, discussion, and deals.[80] Its prominence rapidly matched that of the older Union League. When the federal Industrial Commission and the Commission on Industrial Relations held sessions in Philadelphia during their 1899 and 1914 hearings, testimony was taken at the Manufacturers' Club as a matter of course. Indeed, on the latter occasion, one of its most heralded members was serving as the city's reformist mayor.[81]

By 1910, the club had erected a substantial office building on Broad Street, occupying the top floors for its own use, and continued to blend activism and sociability with fostering business contacts. Soon after, it purchased land for a members' golf course just outside Chestnut Hill and Mount Airy, residential districts that housed hundreds of the city's most successful manufacturing families. Yet signs of a loss of momentum and prestige gathered in the late 1920s. The city's public safety director, charged with enforcing prohibition, had the temerity to raid the club with newspaper reporters and photographers in train. Pictures of members' liquor lockers adorned sarcastic press accounts holding the manufacturing elite up to ridicule. Though charges were eventually dismissed, the club was damaged. Worse, as founding members died and their heirs shuttered failing enterprises and/or moved to suburban havens, membership rolls drooped. Early in the depression, *The Manufacturer* suspended publication; and by the end of the 1930s, the club closed and sold its city building removing all operations to the golf course. With the prestige of business in the nation's political culture frayed, Democrats firmly in power (though not in city government until after the war), and area manufacturing increasingly dominated by branch plants of extra-regional corporations, there would be no more proud Philadelphia delegations to legislative halls, only green fees, cocktails, and grousing in the suburban clubhouse.[82]

The Manufacturers' Club in its prime was an exemplary voluntaristic, regional "peak" institution. It faced both inward toward the city's multiple sectors, seeking to influence local government and establish fruitful business and social linkages among firm owners and their particularized organizations, and outward, toward state and national lawmakers and regulators, toward international rivals and export openings,[83] and with the Bourse, toward building more effective marketing venues for area manufacturers. However, in terms of governance, it was a nullity. The House Committee expelled members not for being bimetallists or Democrats (these were few), or for dealing with unions, but for failure to pay their dues, bar, and meal bills or for outrages against the gentlemanly standards of club behavior (e.g., public gambling or womanizing). The club was an elegant convenience, but little more than the sum of its members' potencies and interests. It served as a platform for organizing strategic consensuses and brilliant banquets, but not a venue for establishing and enforcing rules and routines of business self-regulation. As the relevance of the region and the prospects of members' firms both ebbed, it shed politics and the city and moved quietly into a unitary focus on diversion, simply transporting old assets to a new location.

Not all localized trade organizations were as limited as these three Philadelphia institutions, however. At Grand Rapids, the furniture manufacturers' association long managed a sturdy labour bureau, controlled poaching and wage rates, and excluded unions, yet also created a durable marketing wing, battled railways effectively over rates, and instituted a cooperative warehousing auxiliary for storing goods awaiting transit. It as well set the pace for establishing trade terms that other area furniture trades mirrored and fought the Federal Trade Commission and the Department of Justice to a standstill when its collective activities were challenged through indictments and trial proceedings in the 1920s.[84]

Why was this organization so much more powerful and extensive than those in the Quaker City? Three reasons seem most substantive. First, Grand Rapids furniture companies were makers of styled, bulky final goods. Thus, they had serious incentives for reaching out collectively to retailers, in order to bring buyers in the hundreds (eventually thousands) to Grand Rapids to view seasonal novelties from scores of firms, rather than attempting individually to truck samples, miniatures, or photo sets about the nation. Second, the variety of services the association might provide members was thereby enlarged measurably – not just labour relations and expositions to draw buyers, but also shared freight rate negotiations with railroads, and crucially, storage space, both to save individual firms capital expense for warehousing (because furniture "grows" spatially when assembled) and in order to gather carload lots from diverse makers to single destinations, thus enabling use of bulk rail shipment rates. Membership in and loyalty to the association resolved critical, multiple dilemmas for owners and managers. Third, Grand Rapids was a city "built on wood"; a monoculture district whose furniture trade was its heartsblood, and it faced rival furniture concentrations in a dozen other cities. This singular sectoral commitment reinforced a sense of collective mission, fashioned tools for competitive advantage, and thus helped generate a willingness to accept rules of trade behavior that no Philadelphia association was able to devise and enforce.[85]

A second cluster that managed its collective affairs more assertively and collegially in this era than did Philadelphia's associations was the complex of machine tool builders in Cincinnati, Ohio. Led initially by a quietly charismatic proprietor who had sponsored enterprise starts by a number of his skilled workers,[86] Queen City tool specialists created a local organization in the 1890s. It quickly metamorphosed into the National Machine Tool Builders Association, while Cincinnati builders retained tight linkages to the local branch of the NMTBA and inaugurated a shared marketing venture that sought to supply major, new metalworking plants with arrays of planers, lathes, slotters, millers, etc. that various area specialists could make to specifications rapidly and economically. Through the NMTBA branch, tool builders defeated unions and used its labour bureau to secure skilled operatives. Through collaboration with the University of Cincinnati, they extended apprenticeships into a novel shop and classroom, cooperative engineering training programme. Through the marketing arm, they snared heavy orders from the burgeoning automobile sector for standard and specialized tools. And through the NMBTA, they defied antitrust law and collectively refused to cut prices when tool demand collapsed in the 1913–14 recession and the small and large depressions of 1920–22 and 1929–40.[87]

Here again were sectoral incentives for collective action beyond the realm of labour matters, though they were distinct from those in furniture, as was their enclave district's regional status. Cincinnati's tool companies were specialized startups or spin-offs from the first cadre of post-Civil War generalist builders. Each focused on a specific class of machine tools (lathes, planers, etc.), making collective searches for sales to metalworking corporations using a wide variety of tools a plausible tactic.[88] Their trade was heavily cyclical, accelerating beyond capacity in economic upturns and dropping near zero during recessions. This uncertainty made contracting out sensible in rush periods. As price cuts would not generate orders in slack times, informal or covert/illegal covenants to hold fast to published list prices endured, whereas firms serially hiked list charges when demand rose, thus building profits ploughed into reserves to sustain them during "famines".[89] These shared understandings, the pattern of specialization, the spatial concentration of enterprises, and their particular genealogy all contributed to a climate of multilateral machine tool collaborations, manifested through a variety of institutions.

Philadelphia's metalworking and textile firms were differently positioned. Some in each class made final consumer or capital goods for sale to retailers or clients (carpets, hosiery, tools, engines, locomotives), whereas many fashioned intermediate goods for further processing (yarns, fabrics, castings, machine components), and yet others offered auxiliary services (dyeing, patternmaking). Unlike furniture or machine tools, where almost all firms faced outward toward a "common" market, Philadelphia's textile and metal companies had radically differentiated market arenas – from jobbing machine shops servicing neighbourhood tool or lamp makers to Baldwin forging its way through global openings for locomotive sales, from yarn and dyeing firms feeding regional worsted or carpet weavers to hosiery and lace mills striving to establish national brand names. These lines of differentiation permitted supple production linkages in a profoundly interactive district, but at the same time obstructed effective, multidimensional trade governance. The city's immense scale and diversity gave its Manufacturers' Club prominence and political clout for a generation, but may also have brought attention to issues at so high a level of generality as to blur the perception of specific sectoral concerns.[90] (Though anti-collaboration statutes were hardly trivial, they did not bar business collectivism where a clear definition of shared interests could be articulated that did not rig competition.) In consequence, Philadelphia manufacturers exemplified Powell's "partial and fragmented governance", creating multiple institutions of private ordering that in time gave way to a successor set of equally-partial and fragmented public and hybrid institutions, whose capacities to manage urban industrial restructuring in the post-1945 environment ultimately proved just as limited.

Conclusion

Howell Harris is surely correct in his above-noted assertion that "employers' associations are almost as neglected by . . . historians as are the kinds of firms that joined them". He has also argued that, placed in an international comparative context, "the United States stands out as having the least collectivist employer behavior".[91] Why? On the first count, credit may be placed to business and industrial scholars' relentless attention to the nation's largest corporations and *their* associations (e.g., AISI). As the research ledger is gradually being balanced by increased attention to non-elite firms, sectors outside the mass production mainstream, and more complex and/or secondary industrial cities (Cincinnati and Grand Rapids *vs.* Pittsburgh and Detroit), a fuller understanding of business collectivism should soon be feasible. To Harris's second claim, one might add, "but not for want of trying". As this essay has suggested, manufacturers were prodigious institution builders. Indeed, two surveys in the late 1930s counted over 9,000 active local/regional, state, and national business associations, 2200 of them in manufacturing, half of which were local.[92] Yet more often than not, these organizations were ephemeral or ineffectual, especially along parameters of trade governance. So, again, why?

New institutional theorists have illuminated the deficiencies of universalizing economistic explanations, while comparative historians' analyses of American exceptionalism suggest that differing entrepreneurial cultures and legal frameworks were salient.[93] Yet the latter's accounts are pitched at the national level, whereas governance struggles in this era were commonly sectoral and local/regional in character. There may well have been differing constructions of an "entrepreneurial culture" in Philadelphia, Chicago, and St. Louis (or at Lyon, Paris, and Lille), and spatially-varied degrees of state insertion and structuring, given the disjointed American political system. Moreover, as this chapter suggests, the situational characteristics of sites and sectors were relevant to the outcomes of efforts to craft institutions and governance mechanisms. Encountering this diversity, which institutional theory is beginning to embrace and engage, makes it difficult to accept explanations that ring the chimes of individualism and antitrust and expect that the matter has been resolved. If there is not yet an adequate research base on which to frame a more nuanced account of trade bodies and their roles in both industrial districts and the larger political economy, it may be also too soon to accept the 'least collectivist . . . behaviour' label. Insofar as issues of interfirm collaboration have been for some years hotly debated in the business press and among policy analysts, advancing research along these lines may prove useful both for enriching our historical understanding and for appreciating the regional dimensions of constructing "comparative advantage" within and among nations.

Finally, though it has been elided here, the longer transition from institutions of private to those of public ordering in the American political economy, however disjointed, contradictory, and incomplete it might be, may be further unpacked by attention to meso-level organizations and local/regional transformations. So long as research and analysis focuses on hypostasized firms, markets, and national states, the complex and uncertain dynamics of regional structuration, the institutions that were both media for and outcomes of restructuring and the particularities of place and practice that generated unanticipated consequences of programmatic interventions will rest as background clutter for simplified, naturalistic, and linear tales of advance and decay. To tell these more elaborate and contingent tales, an imaginative fusion of speculation, theory, and empirical research will be necessary. Such a challenge, in the present context, seems well worth accepting.

Notes

1 The pivotal study in this vein is Alfred Chandler, *The Visible Hand*, Cambridge, MA, 1977. For high-tech, see Manuel Castells, ed., *High Tech, Space, and Society*, Beverly Hills, CA, 1988.
2 Howell Harris, 'Getting It Together: The Metal Manufacturers' Association of Philadelphia, *c.* 1900–1930', in Sanford Jacoby, ed., *Masters to Managers*, New York, 1991, 115, 116.
3 Michael Porter, *The Competitive Advantage of Nations*, New York, 1990, 29, 62–63.
4 These institutions included regional port and transit authorities, the Philadelphia Industrial Development Corporation, Pennsylvania Economy League, regional and city planning agencies, etc.
5 See S. Brusco, 'The Emilian Model: Productive Decentralization and Social Integration', *Cambridge Journal of Economics* 6(1982); Ronald Dore, *Taking Japan Seriously*, Stanford, CA, 1986; Michael Piore, 'Work, Labor and Action: Work Experience in a System of Flexible Production', working paper, Economics Department, MIT, 1990; M. F. Raveyre and Jean Saglio, 'Les Systems industriels localises: elements pour une analyse sociologique des ensembles de P. M. E. industriels', *Sociologie du Travail* 2(1984); Charles Sabel, 'Flexible Specialization and the Re-Emergence of Regional Economics', in Paul Hirst and Jonathan Zeitlin, *Reversing Industrial Decline*, Oxford, 1989.
6 Alfred Marshall, *Industry and Trade*, London, 1919, and Allyn Young, 'Increasing Returns and Economic Progress', *Economic Journal* 38(1929): 527–42. For a post-World War Two example of research that deals with sectoral external economies in a dynamic of increasing placelessness, see Richard Langlois, 'External Economies and Economic Progress: The Case of the Microcomputer Industry', *Business History Review* 66(1992): 1–50.
7 The multi-plant national corporation exhibits further patterns and variations, but these are largely extraneous to this assessment of industrial districts, for their relationships annihilate space or convert distance effects into an internalized 'virtual locality' such as in the basic steel and fabrication divisions of U.S. Steel through the 1960s. Governance refers to cross-firm institutions, in the steel case, the American Iron and Steel Institute, for example. See AISI papers, Archives, Hagley Museum and Library, Wilmington, DE.
8 For details, see National Industrial Recovery Administration, 'Hearing on the Special Tool, Die & Machine Shop Industry', October 1, 1934, Record Group 9, NIRA Records, Box 7243, National Archives, Washington, DC. Detailed discussions of parts outsourcing occur regularly in *American Machinist* and *Machinery*, core trade journals, during the later 1910s and 1920s.
9 NIRA Hearing transcript, 5–9. Even as auto manufacturing plants were sited far from the Detroit area by the 1930s, local tool and die firms secured corporate contracts to make and ship their requisite tooling.
10 See John Brown, *The Baldwin Locomotive Works*, Baltimore, 1995. Baldwin in the later nineteenth century did contract locally for parts work, but its commitment to precision and control led it toward substituting 'build' for 'buy' decisions steadily, except for highly-standardized components. On its

in-house work, as Brown documents extensively, Baldwin pursued the practice of internal contracting, thus in a sense, creating its own mini-industrial district among its 8–11,000 employees. Plainly, major corporations outside substantial urban agglomerations (e.g., National Cash Register at Dayton, Ohio or Cambria Steel at Johnstown, PA) could have been making 'pure' market decisions, since they would be less likely to have an array of adjacent specialists comparable to those present in large cities.

11 On shipbuilding, see Thomas Heinrich, *Ships for the Seven Seas*, Baltimore, 1997, and Sun Ship Co., outgoing order letter copybooks, Archives, Hagley Museum and Library; for nonferrous matters, see *Metal Industry* (1908–22), monthly market reports for Waterbury, New Britain, and Bridgeport, passim. Similar contracting for the use of facilities at local, competitive firms in Philadelphia textiles has been noted in my *Proprietary Capitalism* and *Figured Tapestry*.

12 Reciprocity and trust would be indicated in part by specifications for goods ordered. Basic dimensions and sketches would presume that the contractor knew best how to fashion the items required, whereas explicit details as to machine sequencing, gauge-checking, etc. would suggest a low level of confidence and reciprocal respect. For a perspective that regards trust as a far more general problem in industrial organization, see Andrew Sayer and Richard Walker, *The New Social Economy*, Cambridge, MA, 1992, Ch. 3.

13 In one German-rich neighborhood, known as Brewerytown, more than a dozen beer makers concentrated their plants in the later nineteenth century, but as each firm 'sailed on its own bottom', there was no place for productive interaction, save in futile and weak opposition to the advancing forces for Prohibition. For their part, city bakeries divided into neighbourhood suppliers, often with ethnically-distinct product lines, a handful of chain-store suppliers (in Philadelphia, Friehofer's), and a very few national concerns focused on baked 'durables' (i.e., National Biscuit).

14 Particularly in bulk food processing (meat, flour), electrical machinery and products, chemicals and petroleum flow production, bulk metals (steel, aluminum, copper), and transportation equipment (esp. autos). See Chandler, *The Visible Hand*, Cambridge, MA, 1977.

15 Philip Scranton, 'Diversity in Diversity', *Business History Review* 57(1991): 27–90.

16 As noted above in regard to the AISI, this formulation does not preclude similar organization on national or regional levels by major, bulk or mass production corporations. In Detroit, for example, the auto-industry-led Employers' Association of Detroit was a powerful anti-union force for decades. Yet, unless the notion of an industrial district be stretched so far as to eradicate its utility, the EAD must be seen as an extension of corporate standard practice in the nearly universal context of American business's hostility to all forms of labor organization. On the EAD, see Steve Babson, *Working Detroit*, New York, 1984, and Nelson Lichtenstein and Steven Meyer, eds, *On the Line*, Urbana, IL, 1989. For American employers' durable hostility to unions, see Sanford Jacoby, 'American Exceptionalism Revisited: The Importance of Management', in *idem.*, ed., *Masters to Managers*, NY, 1991, 173–200.

17 This is a 'subjective' roster based on my research over the last five years. It is neither exhaustive nor prescriptive.

18 Again, full specification of the achievements and failures evident along these lines in differing locales cannot here be developed. The larger argument, explored in several of my recent papers, and hinted at below, is that sectoral characteristics and development dynamics defined a highly-differentiated array of collective services that governance institutions could (or in failure cases, could not) provide for district firms. See Scranton, 'Supple Cities', paper presented at SHOT conference, Uppsala, Sweden, 1992, and 'The Legacy of Specialization', *New Jersey History* (forthcoming 1994).

19 The scattered-site regional planting of cotton mills in the Piedmont of North and South Carolina, Georgia, and Alabama did not generally involve production linkages among firms, though these did develop in the twentieth century at significant nodes of concentration near Charlotte and Greensboro. The labour history emphasis of much recent work on southern textiles, and the aggregation style of economic historians' analyses leaves ample room for researchers to explore interfirm relations as Southern firms moved beyond bulk staples into more styled fabric trades in the 1920s and after. Earlier, independent spinning mills often supplied knitting or weaving yarns to mid-Atlantic specialists. In any event, Southern textile firms did form trade organizations to combat labour organizers, factory regulation, and promote their growing prowess at cotton expositions at Atlanta and elsewhere before 1900.

20 Classically, the Chicago trades featured specialist firms that made frames, others that added carvings, companies that made springs and underwiring, and final assemblers who gradually shifted from using locally tanned leather to buying-in styled fabrics from Philadelphia and, for silk, Paterson. A few also built hall stands and bizarre chairs using 'waste' horn from the stockyards as basic raw materials. See Sharon Darling, *Chicago Furniture*, New York, 1984.

21 This sector is the one subject of Regina Blaszczyk's University of Delaware dissertation, 'Imagining Consumers: Manufactures and Markets in Ceramics and Glass, 1865–1965', 1995.

22 George Wing, 'The History of the Cincinnati Machine Tool Industry', DBA diss., Indiana University, 1964.

23 Allen Scott, *Metropolis: From the Division of Labor to Urban Form*, Berkeley, CA, 1988. The transfer of the film industry from the east coast to Los Angeles added another skill-intensive, product-diverse trade to the areal manufacturing complement, one that moved rapidly into a variant on oligopoly and Hounshell's 'flexible mass production,' before disaggregating radically in the post-World War Two era. See Michael Storper and Susan Christopherson, 'Flexible Specialization and New Forms of Labor Market Segmentation: The Motion Picture Industry', UCLA Institution of Industrial Relations, Working Paper 105, 1986.

24 Again, the latter doubtless provided electrotypes and catalogues for advertising by clothiers and jewelers, but these were trivial rather than propulsive interactions.

25 Charles Washburn, *Industrial Worcester*, Worcester, MA, 1917.

26 Some also delivered regular publications, either as annual volumes or as regional trade journals.

27 On the PA Manufacturers' Association's provision of such services, see J. Roffe Wike, *The Pennsylvania Manufacturers Association*, Philadelphia, 1960.

28 For example, in 1900, Philadelphia's Manufacturers' Club hosted meetings of the Eastern Bar Iron Assn., the Foundrymen's Assn., the Stove Manufacturers' Assn., the Philadelphia Shoe Exchange, the Shoe-Last Manufacturers' Assn., the Carpet Manufacturers' Assn., the Shoe Manufacturers' Assn., the Philadelphia Oil Association, among others. See *The Manufacturer* 13(Feb. 1, 1900) 53.

29 Obviously, this relative ease of access did not guarantee the efficacy of the relations and organizations established.

30 See Chandler, *The Visible Hand, passim.*

31 Clearly this venue would have had little magnetism for sectoral concentrations whose products were relatively uniform, as for example, meatpackers in Omaha or Kansas City. Instead, futures markets for pricing anticipated flows of staple goods were fashioned, most crucially through the Chicago Board of Trade. See William Cronon, *Nature's Metropolis*, NY, 1992, Ch. 3.

32 Basement floors were outfitted for full-power demonstrations of tenants' machines, while upper story office spaces had huge windows to provide ample lighting for buyers' scrutinizing fabric sample books and the like. The site was a half-block from Independence Hall on South Fifth Street, near the heart of the wholesaling district and within easy walking distance of downtown hotels, the main Broad Street railway station and the Delaware River docks. It has been recently 'recycled' as a shopping and cinema complex. It was formally opened at the close of December 1895 (*Public Ledger Almanac for 1897*, Philadelphia, 1896, 59.).

33 *The Bulletin 1939 Almanac and Year Book*, Philadelphia, 1939, 296.

34 The Commercial Museum is presently the subject of a dissertation in progress at the University of Pennsylvania, under the supervision of Prof. Walter Licht. It opened on June 1, 1896, and was entwined with the university, while being financially supported by business users, municipal and state appropriations, and rental fees for its exhibition halls. (*PLA for 1898*, 63; *The Bulletin 1939 Almanac*, 287.)

35 For expositions and the Merchandise Mart, see Sharon Darling, *Chicago Furniture: Art, Craft, and Industry, 1833–1983*, New York, 1984, 63–64, 292–94.

36 For reports of local association meetings in the metal trades, see *Metal Industry* and *Iron Age, c.* 1905–1930, as well as the journals of the Engineer's Club of Philadelphia, the Engineering Society of Western Pennsylvania, and the St Louis Engineer's Club (Library of Congress).

37 However, regional branch staff could intimidate member firms inclined to break solidarity in strike situations and reach separate settlements that would acknowledge union representation. A well-documented case of staffers' unspecified threats accomplishing this end occurred in Providence in 1917. See Robert McWade to Secretary of Labor William Wilson, May 29, 1917, Federal Mediation and Conciliation Service File 33/441, RG 280, National Archives.

38 In his forthcoming study of the MMAP, Howell Harris of the University of Durham (UK) ably documents the conflicting pressures and initiatives that flowed from metal trades firms' simultaneous membership in the NMTA or NFA and the regional metal trades group.

39 Key works include Emmett Naylor, *Trade Associations: Their Organization and Management*, New York, 1921; U.S. Department of Commerce, Bureau

of Foreign and Domestic Commerce, *Trade Association Activities*, Washington, DC, 1927; Edgar Heermance, *Can Industry Govern Itself?: A Study of Industrial Planning*, New York, 1933; Simon Whitney, *Trade Associations and Industrial Control*, New York, 1934; and *Trade Associations and Business Combinations*, Proceedings of the American Academy of Political Science, 11:4(1926), New York, 1926.

40 For more on these issues, see Leonard Lynn and Timothy McKeown, *Organizing Business: Trade Associations in America and Japan*, Washington, DC, 1988, 45–50.

41 In large part because their records are either guarded, destroyed, or heavily culled before being committed to the hands of archivists. The overhanging presence of U.S. antitrust legislation, which made illegal many of the practices such associations laboured to establish, has made inquiry into their efforts highly problematic. Work in progress by Gerald Berk, University of Oregon, undertakes to remedy this defect. See Berk, 'Communities of Competitors: Open Price Associations and the American State, 1911–1929', Cambridge University ESRC Center for Business Research Working Paper, 1995.

42 Outside manufacturing there were scores more of these national trade associations, among for example dry goods retailers, grocers, electric power companies, wholesalers, railroads, et al.

43 The records of all three institutions are held at the Hagley Museum and Library Archives.

44 For a critique of the Webb-Pomerene corporation, Copper Exporters, as a shadow international cartel immune from antitrust law, see Whitney, *Trade Associations and Industrial Control*, 88–94.

45 Examples being the Textile Manufacturers' National Bank, the Philadelphia Textile School, Cincinnati's Batelle Institute, and trade supported research and training at universities, including the early and widely-copied cooperative engineering program at the University of Cincinnati, or the Industrial Research Unit at the University of Pennsylvania's Wharton School.

46 See Walter Powell and Paul DiMaggio, eds, *The New Institutionalism in Organizational Analysis*, Chicago, 1991; Sharon Zukin and Paul DiMaggio, eds, *Structures of Capital*, New York, 1990; and Michael Best, *The New Competition*, Cambridge, MA, 1990.

47 See Powell and DiMaggio, 'Introduction', *The New Institutionalism*.

48 See Powell, 'Expanding the Scope of Institutional Analysis', and W. Richard Scott, 'Unpacking Institutional Arguments', in *ibid*. Quote from Scott, 171. Anthony Giddens' structuration theory has emerged serially over the last fifteen years. Key texts include *The Construction of Society*, Berkeley, CA, 1984, and *The Consequences of Modernity*, Stanford, CA, 1990. For a reprise of Giddens' work, see Ira Cohen, *Structuration Theory*, New York, 1989.

49 Powell, 'Expanding', 189, 196, in *The New Institutionalism*. See also Philip Ethington and Eileen McDonough, 'The Eclectic Center of the New Institutionalism', *Social Science History* 19(1995): 466–77, for an introduction to five recent studies, all in a political vein.

50 This is evidently the case with trade associations, and the local-state-national governmental divisions may also echo patterns at the level of the firm.

Plainly there are local enterprises and national corporations in manufacturing but few industrial operations that would restrict their activities within state boundaries. However, in contexts of state-level regulation, there were state-confined service sector institutions in banking, insurance, real estate, law, and medicine, at least until recent deregulation and restructuring arrived.

51 Though underspecified, the term 'open system' is a standard element in the rhetoric of the new institutionalists, as even the most casual perusal of the Powell and DiMaggio collection reveals. For the notion that all historical processes are open systems, i.e., underdetermined and interactive processes not reducible to scientific containment and predictive reliability, see J. H. Hexter, *The History Primer*, New York, 1971.

52 Andrew Shonfield, *Modern Capitalism*, Oxford, 1965.

53 Herbert Kitshelt, 'Industrial Governance Structures, Innovation Structures, and the Case of Japan', *International Organization* 45(1991):453–493, quote from 453. For a different, and in part complementary perspective, see Giulio Sapelli, 'A Historical Typology of Group Enterprises', in David Sugarman and Gunther Teubner, eds, *Regulating Corporate Groups in Europe*, Baden-Baden, Germany, 1990, 193–216. In this volume, Gaetano Vardaro scores the tendency of industrial relations scholars 'either to ignore the forms of employers' collective organizations or to regard them merely as a reaction to trade unions', (217) an important observation indeed. For a far less satisfactory treatment of governance in the U.S. and German machine tool industries, see Gary Herrigel, 'Industry as a Form of Order', in Eckhardt Hildebrandt, ed., *Betriebliche Sozialverfassungen*, Berlin, 1991.

54 Charles Perrow, *Complex Organizations*, 3rd. edn., New York, 1986; and idem., *Normal Accidents*, New York, 1984; and idem., 'Economic Theories of Organization', in Zukin and DiMaggio, *Structures of Capital*, 121–152. As Kitschelt summarizes: 'In loosely coupled systems, each step or component of production is separated from every other step in space and time. In tightly coupled systems, there are close spatial and temporal links . . . Complexity refers to the pattern of causal interaction among system components. In systems with linear interaction, an element A causes B, but B has no causal impact on A. In systems with complex interaction, elements influence each other mutually . . . the more that elements engage in circular causal interaction, the more difficult it is to understand the system's operation, to learn from feedback signals, and therefore to keep the system's outputs under control' ('Industrial Governance', 461).

55 Kitschelt, 'Industrial Governance', 463–68. It is in the fourth of these classes that Perrow identifies the dynamics that lead to his specification of 'normal accidents' in nuclear power or space flight, and by retrospective extension, makes intelligible the sixty year struggle of U.S. railroads to elaborate adequate organizational forms at the level of the firm and the system as a whole. Here major state interventions are almost universal.

56 Scott, 'Unpacking', in Powell and DiMaggio, *New Institutionalism*, 179–80.

57 Sanctions are a very touchy matter in the context of American law regarding trade organizations. In Philadelphia textiles and metalworking, firms could be and were expelled from associations for violating key policies (especially in labour affairs) or failing to pay dues and assessments, but fines or 'forfeit' deposits were illegal. As all such groups were voluntary, it was

self-lacerating to dismiss members and far more effective to attempt to offer valued services, while working to exercise peer pressure to enhance membership numbers and persuade firms to adopt common practices.

58 See Edward Lorenz, 'Trust, Community and Flexibility: Toward a Theory of Industrial Districts', paper presented at 'Pathways to Industrialization and Regional Development in the 1990s', UCLA, 1990; *idem.*, 'Neither Friends nor Strangers', and Diego Gambetta, 'Can We Trust Trust?', both in Gambetta, ed., *Trust: Making and Breaking Cooperative Relations*, Oxford, 1988. Trust was exemplified in Philadelphia by situations in which a firm's plant was disabled by fire or flood and sectoral colleagues made their machinery or capacity available so that contracts might be filled, rather than seeking out the afflicted company's clients as substitute suppliers.

59 Were it not for such confidence in others' skills and expectations of reciprocity, it would have been implausible for Philadelphia weaving firms to subcontract dyeing to outside specialists, and for dyers to expand or update their capacity in expectation that satisfied clients would continue to send them work. Relations between metal fabricators and founders or machine shops rested on similar understandings. These assurances were capital-saving at the firm level and enhanced multilateral learning that added to the district's flexible capacities.

60 Lorenz, 'Trust', 11–12.

61 *Ibid.*, 14.

62 Charles Sabel and Jonathan Zeitlin, 'Historical Alternatives to Mass Production', *Past and Present* 108 (August 1985): 133–176. See also their recalibration of this early effort: Sabel and Zeitlin, 'Stories, Strategies, Structures: Rethinking Historical Alternatives to Mass Production', in *idem.*, eds, *World of Possibilities: Flexibility and Mass Production in Western Industrialization*, Cambridge, UK, 1997. There they note that the 'ensemble of regulatory institutions often for long periods was so embedded in the daily flux of business activity as to appear indistinguishable from it. Indeed, there was not even a clear line between regulation through rules and regulation by means of service providing institutions' (25).

63 Scranton, *Figured Tapestry*, New York, 1989, Ch. 6. Skilled labour shortages and the increasing sophistication of TMW's machinery designing led to a rapid succession of larger, faster, and finer-yarn-using knitting machines, *c.* 1910–30. See Textile Machine Works papers, Hagley Museum and Library, especially production ledgers that detail the quick shift from crafting experimental new versions to their production in sizable batches for mill installations.

64 E. E. Greenawalt to W. Kerwin, March 13, 1919, Federal Mediation and Conciliation Service File 120/170, Record Group 280, National Archives.

65 Scranton, *Figured Tapestry*, 364–66.

66 *Ibid.*, 427–49.

67 It must be noted that once nylon seamless stockings became feasible in production terms after World War Two, the entire silk, full-fashioned trade collapsed within a decade. See J. D. deHaan, *The Full-Fashioned Hosiery Industry in the USA*, The Hague, Netherlands, 1958.

68 Also troubling within the later (post-1930) phases of the FHMA's efforts were the large numbers of spin-off, low-end firms started by groups of

displaced skilled workers using adequate but technically-superseded equipment purchased from bankrupt employers. They were intensely hostile to the association and willing to take subcontracted orders from wholesalers at minimal per-dozen rates. Their survivalist ethic, rather than an accumulationist one, furthered the dynamic of discontinuity and decay. Symmetrically, unions whose members took such steps into 'cockroach' entrepreneurship expelled their owners and strove to combat their former colleagues' searches for non-union hands.

69 Howell Harris, 'Getting It Together', 111–131.

70 Nor did it deal in credit reporting, collections, insurance, group purchasing, or materials testing.

71 Harris, 'Getting It Together', 120.

72 On the insignificance of newspaper classifieds, along with state and for-profit employment agencies in this era, see Walter Licht, *Getting Work: Philadelphia, 1850–1950*, Cambridge, MA. 1992.

73 For evidence of NMTA blacklists, see FMCS Files 33/519, 33/678, and 33/1755, NA.

74 Harris, 'Getting It Together', 125, 126.

75 Known union men, of course, were not sent to employers hostile to all labour organizations. I am not certain whether a worker's refusal of a place was noted on his employment record, however.

76 Harris, 'Getting It Together', 129–30.

77 Prof. Harris's full-length study of the MMA and the regional metal trades industries is in revision for Cambridge University Press, and is far richer than this short summary can convey. I have been privileged to read each section in its early and revised versions, but have not here cited or quoted its contents, respecting one of our 'trade customs'.

78 Dobson, Bromley, Dolan, Pollock, Search, Truitt, and Fitler in textiles, Cramp in shipbuilding, Gillinder in glass, Thackara in brasswork, Harrah in steel.

79 The Manufacturers' Club of Philadelphia, *Business Classification of Members*, Philadelphia, 1895, unpaged. Quotes from opening section, 'Its Origins'.

80 *The Manufacturer*, 6–9(1893–1896), passim. The diary of textile manufacturer James Doak (Archives, Philadelphia College of Textiles and Science) confirms that the club was a centre for business deals, political mobilizations, social contacts (and occasional carousing), plus a site for convocations of subsectoral groups when labour conflicts surfaced. Doak, in years after the diary ends, headed the club's legislation committee, and rose to vice-president and president.

81 See Industrial Commission and CIR published hearings volumes. The secretary of the club was the CIR's first witness in 1914; the mayor/member referred to was Rudolf Blankenburg.

82 For the raid, see Philip Scranton and Walter Licht, *Work Sights: Philadelphia, 1890–1950*, Philadelphia, 1986, 135.

83 The club sponsored a long series of international industrial and commercial tours for members, as well as lectures by individuals returning from China, Japan, et al. and by 'experts' in export marketing. It also supported the Commercial Museum heartily, and printed regular reports on its activities in *The Manufacturer*.

84 These activities are documented in the GRFMA Papers, Michigan Room, Grand Rapids Public Library. For discussion see Philip Scranton, 'Manufacturing Diversity', *Technology and Culture* (July 1994): 476–505.

85 Clearly there are far more nuances to the Grand Rapids story than can be conveyed here. However, recent studies suggest that regional furniture employment there in the 1980s matched or exceeded peak levels of the 1920s or 1950s (an indication of regional durability) and document that elaborate contracting networks remain in place. For details, see Scranton, 'Supple Cities'.

86 The reference is to William Lodge, a former machinists' union leader who started his own firm *c.* 1880. After several permutations it became Lodge and Shipley, the city's most prominent lathe makers.

87 See Scranton, 'Diversity in Diversity'. Gary Herrigel, in the essay cited above, seems to have misconstrued key dynamics of the American machine tool sector as he contrasts it with German practice. This evidently was the result of his bypassing an array of rich, but unpublished dissertations on the industry, along with archival records of machine tool firms and NRA files, which document collective agreements for the health of the trade. The standard industry study, is Harless Wagoner, *The U.S. Machine Tool Industry from 1900 to 1950*, Cambridge, MA, 1968.

88 This was not an exclusive pattern by any means, as firms also employed their own 'sales engineers' and shipped sample machines to dealers in major metalworking cities (including San Francisco, and later, Seattle and Los Angeles). Specialist tool builders would keep in stock a few units each of perhaps a dozen 'standard' machine varieties, but most business was based on orders, chiefly for 'specials' produced to match clients' needs or specifications. See George Gray Co. production ledgers, Archives, Cincinnati Historical Society, Museum Terminal, along with Wing, 'Cincinnati', and Wagoner, *Machine Tool*.

89 The Federal Trade Commission suspected the NMBTA of being the organizer of these quickly-spreading 5% or 10% increases and of resistance to price reductions, particularly in the boom and bust sequence, 1917–22. It could not, however, gather sufficient evidence to support a prosecution, and it is possible that tool builders behaved much as did Naomi Lamoreaux's fine paper makers at Holyoke, MA, moving in tandem without central direction. See Lamoreaux, *The Great Merger Movement in American Business*, New York, 1985.

90 This relates to Lorenz's concern that a decentralized trust operates best in smaller communities and that its institutionalization is difficult in fully open contexts where incomers may at little cost defy area norms.

91 Harris, 'Getting It Together', 115, 116.

92 U.S. Bureau of Foreign and Domestic Commerce, *List of State and Local Trade Associations*, Washington, DC, 1937–38; USBFDC, *Trade and Professional Associations of the United States*, Washington, DC, 1942. Pennsylvania alone held 603 local business associations, about half in manufacturing, with 61 national trade organizations headquartered in Philadelphia.

93 See works cited in note 46, and Sanford Jacoby, 'American Exceptionalism Revisited', in *Masters and Managers*, 173–200.

Chapter 3

Electronic component manufacturing and the rise of Silicon Valley*

Christophe Lécuyer

Introduction

The electronics manufacturing complex on the San Francisco Peninsula underwent enormous changes from the 1930s to the early 1970s. Electronics firms in the area employed a few hundred machinists and even fewer engineers in the early 1930s. In the bigger scheme of the total American radio industry, they were marginal. They operated in the shadow of the Radio Corporation of America and other large Eastern firms which had a virtual monopoly on the production and sale of electronic components and systems. Forty years later, the situation had changed dramatically. The Peninsula had become a major industrial centre specialized in electronic components. By the early 1970s, the Peninsula's electronics complex (known by then as Silicon Valley) had a workforce of 58,000 – of which more than half was employed by component firms. The Peninsula was, in particular, the main centre for the development and production of advanced components such as microwave tubes, silicon transistors, and integrated circuits. Because these components were used in virtually every advanced weapon system and were critical to a wide range of industrial goods, the Peninsula's electronics industry became key to the US defence effort as well as central to the political economy of American manufacturing. How did Silicon Valley emerge as a major industrial district? What role did the military and Stanford University play in its formation? How and why did electronics firms in the Valley supersede their Eastern competitors in the component business?

These questions have attracted substantial scholarly attention. Three main theses on the formation and growth of Silicon Valley can be distinguished. In a book and a series of pioneering articles on Stanford's Cold War research programmes and the rise of Silicon Valley, Stuart Leslie argued that the Peninsula's electronics industry grew out of Stanford's teaching and research programmes and benefitted from massive military patronage and procurement during the Cold War. According to Brian Arthur, an economist, the growth of the electronics complex on the Peninsula can be understood as the result of highly contingent events and agglomeration economies. In this view, "key people" such as William Shockley established electronics firms in the area because of "historical accidents". In the second step of the locational process, other tube and silicon corporations were attracted by the presence of these firms. They located nearby to take advantage of the labour expertise and social networks the early firms created. Other companies soon followed. As a result, the electronics industry ended up clustered in locations such as Silicon Valley which were chosen early on in the process.[1]

In her comparative study of Silicon Valley and Route 128, AnnaLee Saxenian has criticized this economic theory. Agglomeration economies, she argued, cannot account for the divergent trajectories of two industrial regions of comparable size, the Silicon Valley and 'Route 128', in the 1980s. Saxenian argued that in order to understand such phenomena one has to take into account regional cultures and organizational forms. Silicon Valley's rise and Route 128's concurrent demise, Saxenian claimed, can be explained by the regions' respective industrial structure. Route 128 has been dominated by large, vertically integrated firms since the postwar period. Silicon Valley, on the other hand, has been characterized since its early days by a highly fragmented and decentralized industrial structure. The Valley was made up of flexible firms embedded in dense regional networks. These firms' key relationships tended to be local. They were engaged in intense direct communication and alternately competed and cooperated with one another. According to Saxenian, these different industrial structures explain why Silicon Valley was more innovative and adjusted more easily to the swift technological and market changes of the 1980s than Route 128.[2]

These interpretations of the Valley's emergence and rapid expansion belong to three different intellectual traditions in the study of industrial clustering. Leslie's Stanford-centred argument resonates with the German school in locational theory (around the work of Johann Christaller and August Lösch) which views industrial clusters as preordained by geographical endowments, shipment costs, and access to skilled manpower. Arthur builds on the work of economic geographers such as Tord Palander, who saw industrial districts as clusters of atomistic firms brought together by historical contingencies and large economic forces. In contrast, Saxenian's work on Silicon Valley belongs to a tradition which emphasizes the social and institutional factors which facilitate external economies of co-location. She draws especially heavily on Michael Piore's and Charles Sabel's flexible specialization argument and more generally on the sociological literature on Italian industrial regions. In this view, industrial districts are made of networks of small and medium-sized firms which produce small batches of output in constantly changing product and process configurations. According to these authors, these homogeneous and highly integrated industrial districts are superior alternatives to autarkic and hierarchical mass production-oriented firms – because they foster technological innovation and adjust rapidly to shifts in technology and markets.[3]

Leslie, Arthur, Saxenian and the three scholarly traditions they represent have taught us a great deal about industrial clustering and the formation of Silicon Valley. I agree with Leslie that military patronage and procurement was critical to the growth of the electronics manufacturing complex on the Peninsula. I partly concur with Saxenian's argument that dense relations among flexible firms in the Silicon Valley gave them a substantial competitive advantage over large Eastern corporations. Finally, I share Arthur's claim that agglomeration economies played a significant role in the Valley's growth. However, their accounts offer a distorted vision of its history. Stanford actually played a modest role in the Valley's formation. While the university-trained microwave engineers made important innovations in microwave tube design, its role in two key industries, power grid tubes and semiconductors, was much more limited, if non-existent, during this period.[4] I want also to show that the Valley's formation was more discontinuous than Arthur claimed. Similarly, interfirm networks did not quite function in the same way as Saxenian argued.[5] More importantly, Leslie, Arthur, and Saxenian have overlooked the skills, technologies, and manufacturing systems which undergirded the region's growth and industrial success. Neither did they analyze the cultural and technological dimensions of the social and business configurations they examined.

In this paper, I am proposing a richer and more complex interpretation of Silicon Valley's formation. This interpretation integrates Leslie's, Arthur's, and Saxenian's contributions into a Marshallian framework. My approach draws on the work of Alfred Marshall, Michael Porter, and John Seely Brown. In his *Principles of Economics*, Marshall sketched an economic and social theory of the emergence and growth of industrial districts. This theory gave a central place to technological skills and manufacturing practices. Marshall argued that groups of skilled workers (along with their political and religious views) are critical to the formation of new industrial complexes. These districts grow and perdure over time because they generate specialized knowledge and attract subsidiary trades as well as a skilled and mobile workforce. In turn, the local knowledge base and the suppliers of specialized inputs bring economic advantages to local firms in the form of external economies. Brown and Porter have recently explored aspects of this framework. Brown focused on the knowledge dynamics of industrial districts. He argued that these regions should be understood as ecologies made of interacting communities of practice. Porter emphasized the role of industrial clusters in competition. According to Porter, intense rivalries within industrial clusters stimulate the formation of new businesses. They also lead to greater productivity and capacity for innovation.[6]

I combine this Marshallian approach with recent concepts and frameworks in the economics of science and technology to understand Silicon Valley. I draw inspiration especially from the work of Nathan Rosenberg, Timothy Brasnahan, and Manuel Trajtenberg and their studies of user-supplier relations and inter-industry linkages. I view industrial districts as complex assemblages of firms, skills, machines, values, and production practices. These districts are built by entrepreneurial and technological groups which come to a previously undeveloped area and set up new industrial firms for a variety of social, cultural, and economic reasons (including the capture of external economies). These new firms and industries depend critically on outside markets. Key to their growth are the relations they establish with external users and the linkages they built with upstream and downstream sectors. Industrial districts also exhibit complex interactions among their various constituents – such as competition, predation, and mutualism. Many different types of industrial complexes can be identified. They range from the highly integrated Italian districts studied by Piore and Sabel to much looser and heterogeneous ones.

I view Silicon Valley in the period under consideration in this paper as a particular kind of industrial district. It was a complex oriented toward the manufacture of advanced electronic components, power grid tubes, microwave tubes, silicon transistors, and integrated circuits. Between 40 and 70% of the Valley's electronics workforce was employed in the component sector between the early 1930s and the late 1960s. Its electronic system sector, with firms such as Hewlett-Packard, remained comparatively small during this period. Because of its specialization in components and the relative weakness of its electronic system industries, the Valley depended almost exclusively on far-away markets. Firms in the Silicon Valley shipped most of their output to the Department of Defense, military electronics system firms, and later consumer-oriented industrial sectors in the East, Midwest, and Southern California. As it grew over time, the Valley became remarkably rich and heterogeneous. It gained many different types of firms, bodies of knowledge, skills, and manufacturing formats (such as flexible specialization and mass production). In particular, the district, which specialized at first in vacuum tubes, acquired new capabilities in the manufacture of silicon transistors and integrated circuits. I also argue that the Peninsula's firms and industries became increasingly interconnected during this period – but not nearly enough to evoke images of holistic entities à la Saxenian.

The emergence and growth of Silicon Valley was a very complex phenomenon shaped by numerous groups as well as economic, social, and political forces. The industrial district was constructed by three successive technological and entrepreneurial groups, radio amateurs, microwave engineers, and silicon technologists. These groups were indigenous to the area or moved to the San Francisco Peninsula in the postwar period. Each group brought with it new design and manufacturing technologies, as well as a distinct culture, style of work, and political

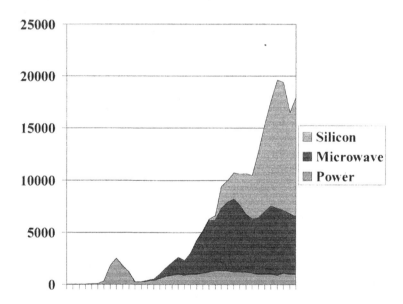

Figure 3.1 Employment in electronic component manufacturing (power grid tubes, microwave tubes, and silicon components) on the San Francisco Peninsula, 1934–1972.

Source: Census of Manufactures

and professional ideologies. In turn, these entrepreneurial and techno-logical communities built three mutually supportive and increasingly interconnected industries: the manufacture of power grid tubes, micro-wave tubes, and silicon components.

The electronics component manufacturing complex on the San Fran-cisco Peninsula was also shaped by military patronage and procurement during World War II and the Cold War. Because of their social and tech-nological innovations, firms on the Peninsula, unlike their East Coast counterparts, were able to capitalize on the growing military demand for very reliable and high performance electronics components during the Cold War. Several major electronics innovations were stimulated by per-ceived problems in meeting the demands of the military for reliability, by the demands of creating a broad consumer base, and by the challenges of commercial production. Thus, when the Department of Defense cut back its component expenditures and radically altered its procurement policies in the early 1960s, the rapid adaptation of a wave of innovations allowed local corporations to redirect their technologies and organiza-tions to commercial markets. As a result, they penetrated a wide range of industrial sectors, transforming the San Francisco Peninsula into the technological centre of American industry.

Amateur radio and the rise of the power grid tube industry

Radio amateurs played a critical role in the formation of the first elec-tronic component industry on the Peninsula, power grid tube manufac-turing. The Bay Area was one of the main centres for ham radio in the United States in the first decades of the twentieth century. By the mid-1920s, the region counted more than 1,200 licensed radio operators. This represented a little less than one-tenth of the total number of radio ama-teurs in America. A number of factors seem to have played a role in the high concentration of radio hams in the area. The region had a strong maritime orientation. San Francisco and Oakland were some of the larg-est seaports on the West Coast. The San Francisco bay also harboured several military bases. Both the Navy and commercial shipping firms relied heavily on radio communication to monitor their operations in the Pacific. As a result, they gave considerable visibility to the new art. In addition to exposing San Francisco youths to the new technology, the Navy and shipping companies employed a significant number of radio operators, some of whom were also involved in amateur radio. The ham radio community in the area was further reinforced by the presence of a small radio system industry. Radio firms such as Federal Telegraph and Heintz and Kaufman provided a source of electronic parts for local hobbyists and strengthened the visibility of radio on the Peninsula.[7]

This vibrant amateur community produced some of the most important power grid tube technologists and entrepreneurs in the area – Charles Litton, William Eitel, and Jack McCullough.[8] It was through amateur radio that these young men acquired their knowledge of electronics and especially short wave radio, the most dynamic field in electronic technology at the time. They also learned to make key components such as power grid tubes for their radio transmitters. These tubes, which generate strong radio frequency signals for long distance transmission, had been developed by General Electric and the Bell Telephone laboratories in the early 1920s. These tubes were the most complex electronic components of the day. They were particularly difficult to make. Their fabrication rested on very complex processes. They had to be baked for hours at a time in order to release gases occluded in their metallic elements. They also required the use of very sophisticated sealing techniques. Through their hobby, Litton, Eitel, and McCullough also acquired the values and practices of amateur radio. Ham radio was a very unusual technical subculture. It was characterized by its strong sociability, its egalitarian and democratic ideology, the value given to ingenuity and innovation, and a mix of competitiveness and information sharing.[9]

After a stint at Federal and Heintz and Kaufman, Litton, Eitel, and McCullough started specialty tube-related businesses, Litton Engineering laboratories and Eitel-McCullough (Eimac), in the early and mid-1930s.[10] Establishing electronics businesses amid the Great Depression was a highly risky, if not foolhardy, undertaking. The entrepreneurs faced a very unpropitious environment. The markets for transmitting tubes shrank in the early 1930s. Furthermore, RCA, General Electric, Western Electric, and Westinghouse controlled most patents in electronics and thoroughly dominated the main markets for power tubes. To survive in this inauspicious environment, the entrepreneurs followed a very similar approach. They focused on niche markets which large East Coast firms did not fully control. To compete in these markets, they emphasized quality, customer service, and technological innovation. They introduced a series of products which met the multifaceted needs of their customers. They also adjusted flexibly to new business opportunities and exploited them aggressively. In keeping with the ham radio ideology of cooperation, these men also colated closely. For example, Litton gave the drawings of his tube-making equipment at no cost to Eitel and McCullough when they started their own business.[11]

While Litton specialized in power tube development and the production of tube making equipment, Eitel and McCullough oriented their firm toward the manufacture of transmitting tubes for radio amateurs. This orientation toward ham radio put Eimac on an unusual technological and business trajectory. Radio hams were the most demanding users of power tubes. They applied very high voltages to their components to increase the power output of their transmitters. Ham radio operators also required tubes which could operate efficiently in the short wave portion of the radio spectrum. To meet the performance and reliability requirements of radio amateurs, Eitel and McCullough developed new processing and manufacturing techniques (using the innovative equipment designed by Litton) and developed a series of high quality tubes. Extending their ham radio line, Eitel and McCullough introduced more powerful tubes for two-way airline radio transmission in 1936.

Because of their unusual reliability and electrical performance, Eimac's tubes gained wide acceptance among radio amateurs and small manufacturers of aircraft radio equipment. To meet the growing demand for their products, Eitel and McCullough hired fellow radio hams and trained them in tube fabrication processes such as glass-blowing, evacuation, assembly, and sealing. As a result of the founders' employment and training practices, Eimac was an unusual firm. It was deeply shaped by amateur radio culture. Great value was given to technical resourcefulness and innovation. Eimac was also characterized by its camaraderie, competitiveness, and democratic ideology.[12]

Because of the unusual reliability of its tubes and the fact that they operated at very high frequencies, Eimac was well positioned to supply advanced tubes for radar development programmes in the late 1930s. It later received a large number of production contracts from the military during World War II. To meet the growing military demand for transmitting tubes in radar and telecommunication systems, the firm converted to volume production. It enlarged its workforce from 17 employees in the summer of 1940 to 3,600 in 1943. To man their plant, the entrepreneurs relied heavily at first on the local pool of ham radio operators and precision machinists (many of these machinists came from Germany and Switzerland). As Eitel and McCullough soon exhausted the supply of radio amateurs on the Peninsula, they increasingly hired women for delicate assembly operations such as the making of grids, plates, and filaments. To train and manage the fast growing workforce, Eitel and McCullough relied heavily on the crew of radio amateurs they had assembled in the 1930s. These men instructed the new hires in the complex techniques of power tube production. They also built large departments around specific manufacturing processes such as pumping, glass-working, and tube assembly.

To scale up production, Eitel and McCullough also reorganized the manufacturing department. They set up a new division to schedule and expedite the flow of materials, tube elements, and semi-assembled tubes throughout the plant. They also mechanized tube production. Until then, power tube manufacture had been a craft-based activity. To mechanize the production of power tubes, Eitel and McCullough hired a group of mechanical engineers with solid experience in machine tool design. They developed special purpose machines to remove bottlenecks in the production process – such as grid making and the evacuation and degassing of tubes. In conjunction with the reorganization of manufacturing, Eitel and McCullough also made social innovations. They set up a profit-sharing programme to give financial incentives to their employees and at the same time stave off organization efforts by San Francisco's unions. As a result of these social and manufacturing innovations, Eimac raised its production rates from a few thousand tubes per month in mid-1941 to 150,000 per month two years later. It emerged as one of the largest tube manufacturers in the United States during World War II. In turn, because Eimac and other firms relied heavily on Litton Engineering's machinery, Litton received very large orders for tube-making equipment and grew substantially – from a few machinists in 1939 to eighty five employees in 1944.[13]

Although Eimac, Litton Engineering, and other vacuum tube firms such as Jennings and ICE (which Eitel and Litton helped establish in the late 1930s) contracted after World War II, these firms contributed to the building of a solid industrial infrastructure on the San Francisco Peninsula. They trained hundreds of operators and technicians in tube fabrication techniques, glass-making, and vacuum processing. They also attracted vendors of specialized materials used in the manufacture of electronic components. Finally, many Eimac machinists established precision machine shops. These shops could machine tube parts and build high precision machinery for other component makers. Thereby, power grid tube manufacturing facilitated the growth of new electronic component industries on the Peninsula in the postwar period.[14]

Cold War manufacturing

Two new specialty component industries, microwave tube and semiconductor manufacturing, emerged on the Peninsula in the second half of the 1940s and the 1950s. These industries were started by groups of Western engineers and physicists, who had moved to the East in the 1930s and early 1940s and returned to the West in the postwar period. Many component entrepreneurs on the Peninsula were originally from the Bay Area and worked on the East Coast in the 1940s and early 1950s. For example, Russell and Sigurd Varian had developed the klystron at Stanford University in the late 1930s, before working for Sperry Gyroscope on Long Island during the war. The Varian brothers moved back to the San Francisco Peninsula and established their own firm, Varian Associates, in San Carlos in 1948. Similarly, William Shockley, a Palo Alto native, who had received a Ph.D. in physics from MIT and co-invented the transistor at the Bell Telephone laboratories in the late 1940s, returned to the Peninsula to start his own semiconductor company, Shockley Semiconductor laboratory, in 1955. In turn, these men attracted Western and midwestern engineers and physicists, who worked for Eastern universities and industrial concerns. This reverse migration of engineers and physicists was motivated by their desire to be closer to their family and, more importantly, live in an environment which they saw as more congenial than the class-conscious and hierarchical East.[15]

These groups of engineers and entrepreneurs brought new competencies, political ideologies, and styles of work to the Peninsula's fledgling electronics manufacturing complex. They introduced very advanced technologies they had helped develop in the East during the war and in the immediate postwar period. They also brought with them their understanding of military contracting and excellent contacts in the armed services and electronic system companies. Finally, the microwave and semiconductor groups brought new technological cultures to the Peninsula. Both groups valued egalitarianism and viewed engineers as independent professionals. However, the microwave and silicon communities differed in other ways. A substantial number in the microwave group had socialist leanings and utopian ideals and longed for a society where the distinction between capital and labour would be abolished. In contrast, the silicon community was meritocratic and resolutely capitalistic.

These groups established two mutually-supportive industries: microwave tubes and silicon components. These industries were oriented almost exclusively toward the military market and saw their expansion fueled by the growing Federal outlays for research and development and weapon system procurement during the Cold War.[16] Microwave tube technologists started the first entrepreneurial wave on the Peninsula in the postwar era – with the formation of Litton Industries, Litton Engineering's sister company, in 1946, Varian Associates (1948), Huggins atories (1948), Stewart Engineering (1952), Watkins-Johnson (1957), and MEC (1959). These start-ups facilitated the entry of older power grid tubes corporations into the microwave tube business. For example, Varian Associates helped Eimac master the new technology of klystron design and processing and establish itself as a major producer of microwave tubes in the early 1950s. These specialty tube firms were followed by a second entrepreneurial wave in semiconductors in the second half of the 1950s and early 1960s. This wave saw the formation of Shockley Semiconductor atory (1955), Fairchild Semiconductor (1957), Rheem Semiconductor (1959), Amelco (1961), and Signetics (1961).[17]

Varian Associates

In order to examine the emergence of the microwave tube and semiconductor industries and their relations with the Department of Defense, I will examine two cases, Varian Associates and Fairchild Semiconductor. These corporations became the largest and most influential firms in the Peninsula's electronic component manufacturing complex. They also offer an interesting window into the mix of values, skills, and business strategies that transformed the San Francisco Peninsula into a major manufacturing centre. Varian Associates, a microwave tube manufacturer, was deeply shaped by California's utopian tradition and the professional ideology of electronics engineering. The Varian brothers were utopian socialists. They had grown up in Halcyon, a utopian and theosophist community on the central California Coast where the means of production were collectively owned and operated. The Varians were interested in recreating aspects of that community in their new corporation. They longed for a system where workers would be in control of their own work and would share in the ownership of the means of production. As a result, Varian Associates was employee-owned – which was very unusual in US electronics in the late 1940s and 1950s. This ownership structure gave a substantial competitive advantage to the firm. It helped bring forth the creative abilities of its engineering and manufacturing workforce and improve its productivity. "Everybody [at Varian]," an engineer recalled, "was a stockholder, or practically everybody. Engineering people had enough stock so that having the company make money was to their personal profit as well as a matter of pride."[18]

Benefiting from the military's rearmament efforts at the beginning of the Cold War, Varian Associates received a contract from the Diamond Ordnance Fuse laboratory to develop an exotic klystron for the fuse of the atomic bomb in 1948.[19] This tube had very unusual reliability specifications. It had to withstand very high shocks and vibrations. The fuse contract was critical for the firm. It helped Varian build an excellent engineering team composed of former Sperry and Raytheon employees. It also enabled the new corporation to gain a unique competence in the design and ultra-clean processing of advanced klystrons. More importantly, this contract gave considerable visibility to Varian in the military sector and transformed it into a key supplier to the Department of Defense.[20]

The Korean War transformed this small laboratory into a much larger enterprise. Varian Associates secured a large number of engineering and pilot production contracts for reflex klystrons and high power klystrons from the Department of Defense and military system contractors in the early 1950s. In keeping with their communitarian ideals, the founders set up new engineering teams to develop these tubes. Like the group that had designed the tube for the fuse of the atomic bomb, these engineering teams were composed of engineers, technicians, and machinists. While the electrical engineers and the physicists on the team worked on the klystron's electrical design, the technicians concentrated on its mechanical construction. Each group was responsible for one specific tube project and dealt directly with the customers. Varian Associates also entered tube manufacture on a small scale during the Korean War. To do so, the firm relied heavily on operators and technicians trained in tube processing by Eimac and other local power grid tube companies.[21]

As a result of the firm's entry into tube manufacture and the expansion of its research and development programme, Varian grew rapidly during the Korean War. By 1953, Varian had emerged as the second largest klystron tube company in the United States and employed more than six hundred engineers, technicians, and operators.[22]

Varian's orientation toward the production of high reliability and high performance components matched well the shift in the military procurement of microwave tubes in the mid-1950s. While the DoD had acquired improved versions of World War II equipment in mass quantities during the Korean War, it increasingly purchased advanced weapon systems in small volumes during the second half of the 1950s. These new systems required high performance and high reliability tubes in relatively small quantities. The growing demand for high quality klystrons offered unique business opportunities to Varian. The firm expanded into volume production of microwave tubes at that time. To do so, Varian transformed itself. It gradually opened its capital to outside investors in order to muster the necessary financial resources that it needed to expand. Varian's founding group also built a flexible manufacturing organization, which met the military demand for complex tubes in short production runs. This flexible production capability and the firm's unique engineering competence helped Varian become the largest micro-wave tube corporation in the nation and supersede established East Coast corporations such as Raytheon, Sperry, and General Electric in the late 1950s and early 1960s.[23]

Fairchild Semiconductor

Unlike Varian and other microwave tube companies which started as contract engineering firms, Fairchild Semiconductor, the most influential semiconductor firm on the Peninsula, had a strong manufacturing orientation from its beginning. It was founded by a group of engineers and physicists (Gordon Moore, Jay Last, Jean Hoerni, Victor Grinich, Julius Blank, Eugene Kleiner, Sheldon Roberts, and Robert Noyce) who had worked for William Shockley at Shockley Semiconductor. These men rebelled against Shockley's heavy-handed management style and set up a new semiconductor operation with financing from Fairchild Camera and Instrument, a medium-sized military contractor on the East Coast, in 1957. The new corporation concentrated on the production of high price and high performance silicon transistors for military avionics system contractors. To do so, it used a new process, solid state diffusion, which had been recently developed by the Bell Telephone laboratories. Unlike Varian, Fairchild had no interest in military research and development contracts – for a number of reasons. Whereas Varian could rely only on the savings of its founders and employees for funds, Fairchild Semiconductor benefitted from Fairchild Camera's generous financing and did not need military patronage to finance research and product development. Furthermore, its founders deemed military research contracts detrimental for a manufacturing organization. Reliance on military research contracts would give the Department of Defense control of the firm's research programme and product line, leading it in directions of direct interest to the military but of little industrial potential. Finally, because of their one- to three-year duration, military research contracts also would restrict the firm's ability to adjust rapidly to new technical and market opportunities.[24]

To engineer and bring diffused silicon transistors to market, Fairchild's founders organized themselves in a loosely integrated fashion reminiscent of Varian's approach to tube engineering (with each founder being responsible for a particular process). They relied on technicians who had been trained in glass-blowing and vacuum techniques at microwave tube companies. They also employed the services of local high precision machine shops for the construction of transistor processing and assembly equipment. These shops had often been established by former Varian and Eimac machinists. Others had been set up by Eastern jewellers and watch makers who had discovered that there was business to be done on the Peninsula and moved to the Bay Area in the 1950s. The presence of a solid component-oriented infrastructure on the Peninsula and the firm's flexible organization helped Fairchild develop its first product at record speed. Fairchild Semiconductor was the first commercial manufacturer to introduce high frequency silicon transistors to the market in 1958. These transistors met a rapidly growing demand for fast silicon components in the emerging field of digital-based guidance and control systems for jet aircraft and missiles.[25]

Fairchild received especially a key contract from Autonetics, the contractor for the guidance and control system of the Minuteman missile. This system had unusual reliability specifications. The Air Force used the Minuteman as a showcase radically to improve the reliability of avionics systems. Up to that time, avionics systems failed on the average every seventy hours, which caused enormous operational and maintenance problems for the Air Force. To solve these problems, the Air Force required that Autonetics improve the reliability of its system by two orders of magnitude. In other words, it specified that the system should have a mean time between failure of 7000 hours. To meet these reliability requirements, Autonetics put enormous pressure on Fairchild to improve the reliability of its devices. Fairchild's first transistor, a mesa double diffused silicon transistor, Autonetics discovered, had major reliability problems. The mere fact of tapping the transistor can with a pencil would produce unstable voltage characteristics and make the transistor unfit for operation. Attracted by the high electric fields at the transistor junctions, the particles shorted the junctions and caused their premature breakdown. A major issue for a start-up depending on a single product, the tap failure problem was made even more acute by the fact that Autonetics demanded very high reliability in components. Solving the tapping problem was imperative. The survival of the company was at stake.[26]

To eliminate tap failures and meet the very high reliability criteria of Autonetics and other avionics manufacturers, Fairchild's engineers, in a burst of technological creativity, developed revolutionary products and processes. Indeed, solving the tap failure problem led Hoerni to make one of the most important innovations in the history of the semiconductor industry. He developed a new process, the planar process. The main characteristic of the planar process was the growing of a silicon oxide layer on top of the silicon crystal. This layer passivated, or electrically stabilized, the crystal's surface and protected the transistor's junctions from outside contaminants. As a result, the planar transistor was much more reliable than its mesa counterpart. Capitalizing on the planar process, Noyce and Last made a second revolutionary innovation. They designed a new silicon device, the integrated circuit, by interconnecting individual planar components such as transistors and diodes in the same wafer through metal wires deposited on top of the silicon oxide layer. Avionics reliability was again the driver of this development.[27]

Because of its advances in design, processing, and manufacturing, Fairchild saw its sales grow explosively from $500,000 in 1958 to $21 million in 1960. The company which had 10 employees on its payroll in October 1957, employed 1400 engineers, operators, and technicians by February 1960.[28]

The success of Fairchild, Varian, and other firms transformed the Peninsula's embryonic industrial complex into a major centre for advanced electronic component manufacturing in the United States. The component industries, which had less than 500 employees on their payroll in 1946, employed more than 11,000 engineers, technicians, and operators by 1960 – two thirds of whom were in the power grid and microwave tube fields. They also gained a central place in the advanced electronic component sector in the United States. By the early 1960s, firms on the Peninsula controlled nearly half of the overall production of microwave tubes in the United States. They also shipped one-fifth of the total output of silicon transistors. Local corporations were particularly strong in the most complex and highest quality components such as travelling wave tubes, high power klystrons, and diffused silicon transistors.

In turn, the rapid expansion of microwave tube and silicon manufacturing further enriched the industrial district. Fairchild Semiconductor and Shockley Semiconductor spun-off various firms that specialized in the production of silicon crystal (Knapic Electrophysics), diffusion ovens, and assembly equipment (Electroglas) in the late 1950s. The success of the microwave tube and semiconductor businesses led also to the formation of the venture capital industry in the area. Five small business investment corporations (SBIC) were established on the Peninsula in the late 1950s. More importantly, two financiers, Arthur Rock and Thomas Davis, who had been involved in the formation of Fairchild Semiconductor and Watkins-Johnson, established Davis and Rock, a venture capital partnership, in 1961. Fairchild entrepreneurs, along with a founding member of Varian Associates, invested in Davis' and Rock's fund. The goal of this partnership and the SBICs was to invest in electronics start-ups in the area.[29]

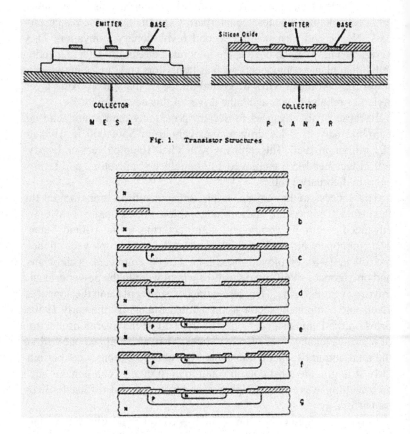

Figure 3.2 The planar process

Source: Jean Hoerni, 'Planar Silicon Transistors and Diodes,' Paper presented at the 1960 Electron Devices Meeting, Washington, DC – October 1960, Bruce Deal Papers, 88–033, Stanford Archives and Special Collections.

The turn to commercial markets

The growth of the microwave tube and semiconductor industries on the Peninsula was brutally halted by major changes in military procurement in the early 1960s. Secretary of Defense Robert McNamara instituted a severe cost reduction programme and restructured military procurement. To reduce costs, the Department of Defense phased out a number of weapon systems, reduced its purchasing of components, and eliminated excess inventories. It fostered competition among military contractors through competitive bidding and second-sourcing. The military also diminished the bargaining powers of its suppliers by requiring access to their accounting books. McNamara's procurement policies had severe repercussions on the electronic component industries on the Peninsula. The military demand for advanced electronic components declined precipitously in the early 1960s. The total military market for silicon transistors, which had grown explosively from $1.8 million in 1955 to $99 million in 1960, fell to $96 million in 1961 and increased at a slow pace thereafter. Similarly the military demand for microwave tubes dropped from $146 million in 1962 to $120 million two years later. The Department of Defense also put growing pressure on tube and semiconductor corporations to submit pricing data, audit their manufacturing costs, and relinquish rights to their processes and production drawings. This cut into the firms' profits and reduced their autonomy vis-a-vis the DoD and military system contractors.[30]

Tube firms on the Peninsula were particularly hard hit by McNamara's reforms. Faced with declining orders, they made substantial cutbacks in their workforce. The cumulative employment of the Peninsula microwave tube industry declined from 7000 in 1962 to 5200 three years later. The crisis was particularly acute at Varian Associates. Because Varian refused to open its books to military auditors, the DoD black-listed the firm, refusing to grant it new research and production contracts. The military forcibly moved tube development teams from Varian Associates to Eimac. It also asked Litton Industries to reverse-engineer Varian's high power klystrons and produce them at a lower cost. As a result of these punitive measures, Varian almost went bankrupt and was forced to layoff half of its tube workforce in 1963.[31]

The 'McNamara depression' deeply transformed the Peninsula's tube industries. It led to a consolidation of the tube sector and forced local firms to diversify into commercial markets. To reverse its sagging fortunes, Varian acquired or merged with various tube operations on the Peninsula, including Eimac, in the first half of the 1960s. It also moved into the design and manufacture of commercial systems to reduce its dependency on military contracting – both through internal R&D programmes and the acquisition of other science-based firms. Varian focused especially on fields in which the government was increasingly investing in the 1960s: research in the physical and biological sciences and, more importantly, health care. Varian built new businesses in NMR spectrometers, clinical linear accelerators, and vacuum systems for semiconductor manufacturing. It also purchased medium-sized computer, scientific instrumentation, and vacuum component corporations to strengthen its presence in the commercial markets. As a result of these acquisitions and vigorous development efforts, Varian became a commercially-oriented firm. By 1966, 70% of its sales were in the commercial sector.[32]

In contrast, semiconductor firms on the Peninsula, which experienced a similar decline in their military sales, developed commercial markets for their own products, silicon transistors and integrated circuits, in the first half of the 1960s. Fairchild Semiconductor pioneered the construction of markets for silicon components in the commercial computer and consumer electronics industries in the first half of the 1960s. The firm did so by adopting a very innovative approach. To learn more about commercial markets and acquire a deep knowledge of system engineering, Fairchild brought the 'customers' into the firm by hiring circuit and system engineers from corporations such as IBM, General Electric, Philco, and Zenith. These engineers were asked to develop a line of transistors and integrated circuits which would meet the needs of commercial users. In conjunction with the development of system-oriented devices, they engineered new applications around Fairchild's products. The firm gave these circuit and system designs at no cost to its customers. For example, application engineers at Fairchild designed an all-transistor television set in 1962 'to demonstrate the feasibility of using transistors in TV'.[33] They built a television prototype which was smaller, more reliable, and had better temperature characteristics than television sets then available on the market. The Fairchild design was widely adopted by the television industry and mass-produced by General Electric, Zenith, and Sylvania.[34]

In conjunction with the development of system-oriented products and the development of new applications, Fairchild scaled up production and drastically reduced prices in order to penetrate the commercial markets. The firm acquired a mass-production expertise by hiring Charles Sporck and other manufacturing engineers from General Electric's capacitor division. These men gradually reshaped the organization and the techniques of production at Fairchild and transformed a small, craft-oriented manufacturer into the first mass-producer of diffused silicon transistors and integrated circuits. The group from GE reorganized the firm's manufacturing department along product lines. They also introduced new production and inventory control techniques to plan, schedule, and expedite the flow of parts through the factory. To further reduce production costs, these men delocalized Fairchild's assembly operations to low labour cost areas. In 1962, Sporck founded a plant in Maine where wages for unskilled operators were half of those in the Bay Area. One year later, the firm established a subsidiary in Hong Kong to take advantage of the territory's cheap labour. These new plants and the mass-production techniques brought from GE helped Fairchild drastically reduce its production costs and meet the price requirements of commercial users. As a result of these innovations in manufacturing and marketing, Fairchild developed vast markets for its components in the computer and consumer electronics industries in the first half of the 1960s.[35]

The commercial markets for integrated circuits were further enlarged and exploited by a new wave of semiconductor start-ups in the late 1960s and early 1970s. Forty-seven semiconductor companies, including Intel, AMD, Intersil, and National Semiconductor, were established on the Peninsula from 1966 to 1972. Most of these firms were founded by former Fairchild Semiconductor employees. Among them were key engineers and managers such as Sporck, Noyce, Moore, and Hoerni. These men left Fairchild to establish their own firms for a variety of reasons. They were interested in exploiting the market and technological opportunities opened up but not fully cultivated by Fairchild. More importantly, they became disenchanted with the corporation and were often eased out of Fairchild Semiconductor by the conflicts that roiled the firm and its parent company, Fairchild Camera, in the late 1960s. Some like Moore were frustrated by the difficulties Fairchild Semiconductor had in transferring new products from R&D to manufacturing.

Others such as Sporck repeatedly clashed with Fairchild Camera regarding the use of Fairchild Semiconductor's hefty profits and the granting of stock options. With these profits, Fairchild Camera acquired troubled corporations instead of reinvesting in the semiconductor business. It also refused to grant generous stock options to engineers and managers whom Sporck saw as critical to the company's future. The crowning event was the management turmoil at Fairchild Camera in 1968 which led to Noyce's and Moore's departure, their replacement by a managerial team from Motorola, and the mass exodus of Fairchild Semiconductor's managers and engineers that ensued.[36]

The formation of new semiconductor firms was greatly facilitated by the Peninsula's growing venture capital and semiconductor equipment industries. The venture capital business rapidly expanded in the area in the late 1960s and early 1970s. No less than thirty new and reconstituted venture capital operations were formed on the Peninsula between 1968 and 1975. This surge in venture capital encouraged the formation of semiconductor start-ups – by assuring potential entrepreneurs that investment backing was available. Venture capitalists also funded many new silicon corporations. For example, Rock played a major role in the financing of Intel and Intersil. The entrepreneurial flourish in the semiconductor business was also made possible by the Peninsula's expanding semiconductor equipment industry. In conjunction with the microwave tube companies' entry into the semiconductor equipment business, new firms such as Applied Materials commercialized critical pieces of equipment which up to that time had been developed and used internally by Fairchild. The commercial availability of diffusion ovens, epitaxial reactors, and novel photolithographic equipment considerably lowered the barriers of entry into the semiconductor business. New corporations could procure them immediately, rather than having to devote considerable engineering and financial resources to duplicate Fairchild's equipment.[37]

While Fairchild had pursued a broad array of technologies and markets in the mid-1960s, its spin-offs concentrated on specific circuit types and user applications. For example, National Semiconductor focused on the low cost production of standard linear and digital circuits for the industrial market. Intel used the new MOS process developed at Fairchild to produce memory circuits for the computer industry. To establish themselves as key players in the silicon business, the start-ups modelled themselves after Fairchild. They were mass production-oriented and relied extensively on low cost labour in South-East Asia. They also adopted and further refined Fairchild's innovative marketing techniques. They built strong application laboratories to develop new markets for integrated circuits in a wide range of commercial sectors. Learning from Fairchild's shortcomings, the entrepreneurs also set up generous stock option programmes to give financial incentives to engineers and middle managers.[38] Because the US market for integrated circuits exploded from $75 million in 1965 to $1.2 billion ten years later, Fairchild's spin-offs grew very rapidly. For example, National employed more than 2000 engineers, workers, and technicians on the Peninsula by 1972. As a result of the explosive growth of National, Intel, Intersil, and other firms, the total semiconductor employment on the Peninsula doubled from 6,000 in 1966 to 12,000 six years later.

The rapid expansion of the silicon industry, in conjunction with the crystallization of the venture capital business, had an enormous impact on the Peninsula's industrial complex. It deeply reshaped the electronics manufacturing complex and transformed it into the 'Valley of Silicon'. The semiconductor industry became the main manufacturing sector on the Peninsula. As a result, tube companies, which had dominated the Peninsula's industrial complex until the mid-1960s, were relegated to a marginal position. They transformed themselves into large suppliers of manufacturing equipment to the silicon industry. For example, Varian, which had developed a small semiconductor equipment business in the early and mid-1960s, made a major thrust into the production of ion implanters and other special purpose machines and established itself as one of Intel's, Fairchild's, and National's most important suppliers in the early and mid-1970s. The expansion of the semiconductor industry and the growth of venture capital firms also altered the institutional and cultural fabric of the Peninsula's electronics manufacturing complex. They unleashed an extraordinary wave of entrepreneurship in a wide range of electronic system industries. They led to the stabilization of incentive structures around stock option plans and encouraged the wide diffusion of the horizontal organizational firms pioneered by Varian and Fairchild. More importantly, the development of new technologies and markets by semiconductor manufacturers transformed silicon electronics into a general purpose technology. It also made of the Peninsula a major technological and commercial centre.

Conclusion

'It seems remarkable to me', William Eitel reflected in 1962, 'that [on the San Francisco Peninsula], off the beaten paths of commerce, grew so many independent new industries, all now of national and international importance'.[39] In the 1960s, the Peninsula was indeed very different from the region Eitel had known as a young radio amateur forty years earlier. By the late 1920s, the Peninsula was home to a handful of radio firms. These firms had a cumulative workforce of a few hundred engineers and operators. Four decades later, the region had become the main centre for advanced electronic component manufacturing in the United States. The formation of this production complex was a contingent and multicausal process. It depended on cross-continental migrations of engineers and scientists and the acquisition of key military contracts which forced local firms to make major process and design innovations. Crucial to the emergence and growth of the Peninsula's electronics manufacturing complex were three technological and entrepreneurial groups: radio amateurs, microwave engineers, and silicon technologists. Each entrepreneurial and technological wave added to, rather than displaced, the existing capabilities and institutions that preceded it. It also facilitated the later emergence and growth of new industries. For example, the skills and capabilities assembled and created by the tube industries were critical for the formation of and early expansion of semiconductor manufacturing on the Peninsula. The electronic component manufacturing complex on the Peninsula was also shaped by major shifts in the demand for tubes and semiconductors brought about by changes in system design, the ebbs and flows of military procurement, and the evolution of international relations.

Component firms in the Silicon Valley grew rapidly and competed successfully with their Eastern counterparts for a variety of reasons. As Arthur and Saxenian argued, agglomeration economies and collaborative practices gave a significant competitive advantage to firms in the Silicon Valley. These corporations benefitted from agglomeration economies generated by the area's increasingly rich industrial environment. The Peninsula's industrial environment provided the capital, facilities, technical and management skills required by start-ups as well as established firms. The specialized nature and collaborative practices of Peninsula firms also helped them compete successfully with their Eastern counterparts. But, unlike what Saxenian claimed, these networks of specialized firms were not the primary catalyst for technological innovation. Rather, they facilitated the entry of new as well as established firms into new businesses.

Agglomeration economies and flexible networks do not solely explain the success of Silicon Valley firms. Because of the district's origins in amateur radio and close ties with utopian communities, firms in the Valley made important management innovations. Technical entrepreneurs on the Peninsula built flat organizations with few hierarchical layers. They granted substantial autonomy to their engineering staff and organized research and development around independent teams. They also gave unusual financial incentives to their employees – through profit sharing, stock ownership, and stock option programmes. Because of these new financial incentives and organizational forms, electronics firms on the Peninsula attracted some of the best design, process, and manufacturing engineers in the nation. These innovations also permitted local firms to organize engineering work in an efficient fashion and to improve employee productivity. Flat organizational structures, profit sharing, and stock option programmes gave them a substantial competitive advantage over their more traditional Eastern counterparts.

Unlike their Eastern competitors, firms in the Valley, whether they were specialty or mass-production oriented, emphasized quality and served the most demanding users. Tube and semiconductor firms on the Peninsula concentrated on the design and production of the highest performance and most reliable tubes, transistors, and integrated circuits on the market. They also addressed the most exacting electronic applications. The area's bias toward quality matched the evolution of the demand for electronic components. For example, the military shifted its procurement of components toward high performance and highly reliable tubes and semiconductors in the mid-1950s. Computer and consumer electronic users required even faster and more reliable components in the following decade. While local firms greatly benefitted from this shift in markets, East Coast corporations, which emphasized cost and manufacturability, lost market share and were often forced to leave the component business in the mid- and late 1960s.

More importantly, firms in the Valley acquired unusual processing and manufacturing competencies. In order to meet the performance and reliability requirements of their customers, power tube, microwave tube, and semiconductor firms in the Valley made major processing and manufacturing innovations. Among the most notable were the development of high vacuum techniques in the power grid tube and microwave tube industries, the invention of the planar process, and the construction of mass production systems for the manufacture of silicon transistors and integrated circuits. These innovations helped them produce very advanced components which Eastern corporations could not fabricate. Unique processing and manufacturing capabilities permitted Silicon Valley firms to produce tubes and semiconductors at higher yields and therefore at lower cost than Eastern suppliers.

The Peninsula's electronic component manufacturing complex and the venture capital industry that emerged from it provided the foundation for much of Silicon Valley's growth in the 1970s and early 1980s. Much of the Valley's expansion during this period was in electronics systems such as computers, communication equipment, scientific and medical instruments. The component industries, especially semiconductor manufacturing, contributed very substantially to the growth of computing and instrumentation in the Valley. Starting in the early 1960s, component firms diversified into these industries. More importantly, the silicon industry provided a very powerful technology around which entirely new products and industries could be created. Ever more powerful and cheaper integrated circuits made possible the design of totally new products, digital calculators, personal computers, workstations, ink-jet printers, and telecommunication equipment. Many of these technological and business opportunities were exploited by new corporations such as Apple, Osborne, Atari, Rolm, and SUN Microsystems.[40]

In addition to the supply of revolutionary components, semiconductor manufacturers contributed to the growth of the electronic system industries in a more indirect way. Fortunes made in semiconductors were partially reinvested in new system ventures. Component firms were also a major source of managerial talent for the system sector. For instance, Michael Markkula, formerly at Fairchild and Intel, became Apple's first general manager and played a critical role in the firm's early growth. Component firms also provided a model for new system corporations. These companies were organized around the culture of innovation and engineering autonomy that had been pioneered in the component industries. They also relied heavily on venture capital for their early financing and gave stock options to most of their employees. Thus, a few radio amateurs tinkering with transmitting tubes in the 1920s gave birth to a remarkably rich and dynamic industrial district in electronics, computing, and telecommunication. In less than half a century, the Peninsula's electronics manufacturing complex became a major industrial and commercial centre. It also reshaped the nation's technological fabric as well as the spatial distribution of skills, knowledge, and economic resources in America.

Christophe Lécuyer postscript

This chapter offers a skill-based interpretation of Silicon Valley's emergence from the 1930s to the early 1970s. It argues that competencies in process development and manufacturing were critical for the growth of several industries in the region: power grid tubes, microwave tubes, and semiconductors. Also essential for the success of Silicon Valley firms was their creation of new forms of venture financing and novel managerial techniques aiming at mobilizing and retaining a skilled workforce. These technological and managerial skills enabled Silicon Valley's corporations to establish themselves in industries originally pioneered on the East Coast of the US. This argument on the early history of Silicon Valley was further developed in my books: *Making Silicon Valley: Innovation and the Growth of High Tech, 1930–1970* (MIT Press, 2006) and *Makers of the Microchip: A Documentary History of Fairchild Semiconductor* (MIT Press, 2010, in collaboration with David C. Brock). More recently, I explored the environmental impact of electronic component manufacturing in Silicon Valley in "From Clean Rooms to Dirty Water: Labor, Semiconductor Firms, and the Struggle over Pollution and Workplace Hazards in Silicon Valley", *Information & Culture*, 52–3 (2017), 304–33.

Notes

* I would like to thank Philip Scranton and the participants in the 'engineering post-war industry' workshop at the Hagley Museum and Library for their comments on this paper. I also gratefully acknowledge the support of the Charles Babbage Institute, the IEEE Centre for Electrical History, Stanford

University, and the Dibner Institute for the History of Science and Technology for the preparation of this essay.

1 Stuart Leslie, *The Cold War and American Science: The Military-Industrial-Academic Complex at MIT and Stanford* (New York: Columbia University Press, 1993); Robert Kargon, Stuart Leslie, and Erica Schoenberger, 'Far Beyond Big Science: Science Regions and the Organization of Research and Development', in Peter Galison and Bruce Hevly (eds), *Big Science: The Growth of Large-Scale Research* (Stanford: Stanford University Press, 1993), 334–354; Stuart Leslie, 'How the West Was Won: The Military and the Making of Silicon Valley', in William Aspray (ed.), *Technological Competitiveness: Contemporary and Historical Perspectives on the Electrical, Electronics, and Computer Industries* (Piscataway: IEEE Press, 1993), 75–89; Robert Kargon and Stuart Leslie, 'Imagined Geographies: Princeton, Stanford and the Boundaries of Useful Knowledge in Postwar America', *Minerva*, 32 (1994), 121–143; Stuart Leslie, 'Electronics and the Geography of Innovation in Postwar America', *History and Technology*, 11 (1994), 217–231; W. Brian Arthur, 'Silicon Valley's Locational Clusters: When Do Increasing Returns Imply Monopoly', *Mathematical Social Sciences*, 19 (1990), 235–251 and 'Industry Location Patterns and the Importance of History', in Arthur, *Increasing Returns and Path Dependence in the Economy* (Ann Arbor: University of Michigan Press, 1994), 49–67.
2 AnnaLee Saxenian, *Regional Advantage: Culture and Innovation in Silicon Valley and Route 128* (Cambridge: Harvard University Press, 1994).
3 Johann Christaller, *Central Places in Southern Germany* (New York: Prentice Hall, 1933); August Lösch, *The Economics of Location* (New Haven: Yale University Press, 1954); Tord Palander, *Beiträge zur Standortstheorie* (Almpvist and Wicksell, 1935); Michael Piore and Charles Sabel, *The Second Industrial Divide: Possibilities for Prosperity* (New York: Basic Books, 1984). Piore's and Sabel's argument draws on 'la théorie de la régulation' and the work of Fréderic Le Play and especially his study of the Parisian luxury trades and other forms of 'fabriques collectives' in the 1860s. For Le Play's discussion of industrial clustering, see Fréderic Le Play, *La Réforme Sociale en France*, volume 1 (Paris: Henri Plon, 1864), 302–315 and *La Réforme Sociale en France*, volume 2 (Tours: Alfred Manne et Fils, 1878), 288–307.
4 Stanford played a more important role in the 1970s and 1980s. For example, its VLSI project led to the formation of MIPS, Silicon Graphics, and SUN Microsystems.
5 The Valley's interfirm networks functioned like Saxenian's 'production networks' in the late 1970s and 1980s – when the region's growing electronic system sector got increasingly tied in with local component manufacturers.
6 Alfred Marshall, *Principles of Economics* (London : Macmillan, 1890); John Seely Brown and Paul Duguid, 'Mysteries of the Region: Knowledge Dynamics of Silicon Valley', in Chong-Moon Lee, William Miller, Marguerite Hancock, and Henry Rowen, eds, *The Silicon Valley Edge: A Habitat for Innovation and Entrepreneurship*, Stanford: Stanford University Press, 2000, 16–45; Michael Porter, *The Competitive Advantage of Nations* (New York: The Free Press, 1990), *On Competition* (Boston: Harvard Business School Press, 1998), and 'Clusters and the New Economics of Competition', *Harvard Business Review*, November-December 1998, 77–90.

7 For a treatment of the radio industry on the Peninsula, see Arthur Norberg, 'The Origins of the Electronics Industry on the Pacific Coast', *Proceedings of the IEEE*, 64 (1976), 1314–1322 and Jane Morgan, *Electronics in the West: The First Fifty Years* (Palo Alto: National Press Books, 1967). For a list of radio amateurs in the United States in the mid-1920s, see US Department of Commerce, *Amateur Radio Stations of the United States* (Washington, DC: US Government Prining Office, 1928).

8 These men had been trained in the mechanical arts and had close ties with the mechanical industries in the Bay Area. For example, Eitel came from a family that had ventured in the design of aircraft engines in the 1910s. His uncle E. J. Hall had established the Hall-Scott Motor Car Company in Oakland, one of the first automotive corporations in the West.

9 For a treatment of ham radio culture, see Susan Douglas, *Inventing American Broadcasting, 1899–1922* (Baltimore: Johns Hopkins University Press, 1987), 187–215 and Clinton B. De Soto, *Two Hundred Meters and Down: The Story of Amateur Radio* (West Hartford, Conn.: American Relay League, 1936). For Eitel's and McCullough's amateur activities, see William Eitel, oral history interview conducted by Arthur Norberg, 1974 and Jack McCullough, oral history conducted by Norberg, 1974, both at the Bancroft Library, University of California.

10 These ventures were financed by the entrepreneurs' savings and local businessmen.

11 The entrepreneurs benefitted from the Bay Area's diversified industrial structure. The region had a strong chemical sector as well as machine tool makers, automotive and aircraft manufacturers, radio companies, and firms specializing in the processing of wood and agricultural products. These industries served mostly local markets in California and parts of Utah. For RCA's patent monopoly, see Robert Sobel, *RCA* (New York: Stein and Day, 1986) and W. Rupert Maclaurin, *Invention and Innovation in the Radio Industry* (New York: The Macmillan Company, 1939). For statistics on power tube manufacture, see Department of Commerce, *Census of Manufacture* (Washington, DC: Government Printing Office, 1931 and 1933). For an analysis of specialty production, see Philip Scranton, *Figured Tapestry: Production, Markets, and Power in Philadelphia Textiles, 1885–1941* (Cambridge: Cambridge University Press, 1989); Scranton, *Endless Novely: Specialty Production and American Industrialization, 1865–1925* (Princeton: Princeton University Press, 1997); Scranton, 'Diversity in Diversity: Flexible Production and American Industrialization, 1880–1930', *Business History Review*, 65 (1991), 27–90.

12 For a history of Litton Engineering, see J. G. Copelin, 'History of Litton Engineering laboratories and Report on Operations for Year 1942', April 19, 1944, carton 1, folder: renegotiation, Charles Litton Papers, 75/7c, Bancroft Library. For Eimac's early history, see 'Tenth Anniversary Edition', *Eimac News*, September 9, 1944, 6–11, collection 739, San Mateo County Museum, Redwood City.

13 David Allison, *New Eye for the Navy: The Origin of Radar at the Naval Research Laboratories* (Washington, DC: Naval Research atory, 1981); Tenth Anniversary Edition', *Eimac News*; Harold Zahl, *Radar Spelled Backwards* (New York: Vantage Press, 1972); Eitel, oral history interview conducted by

Norberg, 65–78; E. Walsh, 'Litton Engineering laboratories: Brief History and General Comments', October 12, 1942, carton 1, folder: renegotiation, Charles Litton Papers, 75/7c, Bancroft Library.

14 Arnold Wihtol, oral history interview conducted by the author, April 3 and April 9, 1996.

15 For the reverse migration of Western engineers to the West after the war, see Arnold Wihtol, oral history interview conducted by the author, March 5, 1996; Dorothy Varian, *The Inventor and the Pilot* (Palo Alto: Pacific Books, 1983).

16 The microwave tube and semiconductor entrepreneurs faced a much more favorable legal and business environment in the postwar period than Eitel and Litton had encountered in the 1930s. The Federal government strictly enforced antitrust laws after the war and forced large firms such as AT&T to sign consent decrees that led to the liberal licensing of their electronic component patents. The courts also developed a much more lenient attitude regarding intellectual property rights during this period. This new legal environment prevented large electronics corporations to block the entry of new competitors through patent lawsuits. It also made possible the massive appropriation of new technologies developed by the Bell Telephone laboratories and other Eastern institutions by the Valley's start-ups. Business conditions became also increasingly propitious in the postwar era. The market for advanced electronic components exploded in the late 1940s and 1950s. The Department of Defense required ever more complex electronic components for its radar, telecommunication, and weapon systems during the Cold War. The explosion of these markets offered substantial business opportunities to new firms. The military also provided considerable help to fledgling electronic businesses through Victory loans and research and development contracts. These loans and contracts provided working capital to start-ups. They also helped new corporations build up their engineering staff, finance research and product engineering, and set up production facilities. For an analysis of changes in intellectual property regimes after the war, see David Hart, *Forged Consensus: Science, Technology, and Economic Policy in the United States, 1921–1953* (Princeton : Princeton University Press, 1998), 84–95.

17 For Varian's assistance to Eimac in the microwave tube field, see Myrl Stearns, oral history interview conducted by the author, November 25, 1996; Eitel, oral history conducted by Norberg; McCullough, oral history conducted by Norberg. Varian, Eimac, and Litton Industries helped attract established electronics corporations in the East and Midwest such as Sylvania and General Electric to the Peninsula. These companies set up their Western microwave tube plants and laboratories in the area in the 1950s.

18 Richard Nelson, oral history interview conducted by Sharon Mercer, 5, Varian Oral History Collection, M 708, Stanford University Archives and Special Collections. For a historical treatment of the Theosophic community in Halcyon, California, see 'The Temple Home Association. Report and Message of the President Read at Last Annual Meeting', *Temple Artisan*, August 1911, 198–201; and 'The Temple Home Association', *Temple Artisan*, May 1918, 331–332, both at the Bancroft Library. See also Robert Hine, *California's Utopian Colonies, 1850–1950* (New York: W. Norton & Company,

1973), 38–57. For Varian's institutional goals and ownership policies, see Russell Varian, 'Outline of Talk before Shareholders' Meeting', December 3, 1951, in folder 28, box 41, series: Russell Varian, Russell and Sigurd Varian Papers, SC 345, Archives and Special Collections, Stanford University; 'Stock Option Agreement', November 30, 1948, folder 11, box 5, series: Varian Associates, Russell and Sigurd Varian Papers, SC 345, Archives and Special Collections, Stanford University; Russell Varian, 'Report on Stock Policies', May 27, 1952, folder 11, box 5, series: Varian Associates, Russell and Sigurd Varian Papers, SC 345, Archives and Special Collections, Stanford University.

19 One might wonder why the founders who had progressive political views accepted such a contract. One can speculate that it was a matter of necessity. The firm had to get government contracts, whatever contracts, to survive. Other factors may have played a role in this decision. The DOFL contract offered challenging technical problems. Finally, the Varian brothers were no Marxist socialists and had little sympathy for the Soviet Union. There is evidence, however, that some members of the group, especially Sigurd Varian, later sorely regretted their involvement in the development of fuses for the atomic bomb.

20 For the fuse contract from DOFL, see Chodorow, oral history interview conducted by Mercer 1989, 16–18; Ginzton, oral history interview conducted by Mercer; 'Minutes of Special Meeting of the Board of Directors of Varian Associates', September 27, 1948, volume 2, box 17, Edward Ginzton Papers, SC 330, Archives and Special Connections, Stanford University; Russell Varian, 'Ten Years Later . . . A New Industry is Born', *Varian Associates Magazine*, September 1958, 10–11, 10, folder 4, box 7, series: Varian Associates, Russell and Sigurd Varian Papers, SC 345, Archives and Special Collections, Stanford University.

21 Varian's founders also established a new organization, the Management Advisory Board (MAB), in the early 1950s. The Board, which was elected by the firm's engineers, technicians, and operators, had the authority to study any problem pertaining to the management of the company. The MAB addressed sensitive issues such as injuries on the job, lay-off policies, and the company's wage structure. Many of its recommendations were adopted by Varian's management.

22 For Varian's contracts during the Korean War, see 'Varian Associates Financial Statements for the 12 Months Ended September 30, 1951', folder: Russell Varian – board of directors, box 6, series: Russell Varian, Russell and Sigurd Varian Papers, SC 345, Archives and Special Collections, Stanford University; 'Financial Statement for the Eleven Months Ended August 31, 1952', folder 19, box 3, series: Varian Associates, Russell and Sigurd Varian Papers, SC 345, Archives and Special Collections, Stanford University; John Clark, 'Current Contracts which Can Support Long Range Development Studies', July 23, 1951, folder: Varian Associates – not classified, box 3, Edward Ginzton Papers, SC 330, Archives and Special Collections, Stanford University.

23 For the evolution of military procurement in the second half of the 1950s and early 1960s, see *Electronics Industry Association Yearbook*, 1964, courtesy of Jay Last. For Varian's manufacturing operations in the mid-1950s, see

anonymous, 'The Jobshop: Where Tubes are Built from Ideas', *Varian Associates Newsletter*, July 1956, 9, folder 1, box 7, series: Varian Associates, Russell and Sigurd Varian Papers; Wihtol, oral history interview conducted by the author, April 3 and April 9, 1996.

24 For Fairchild Semiconductor's early history, see Lécuyer, 'Fairchild Semiconductor and its Influence', in Chong-Moon Lee, William Miller, Marguerite Hancock, and Henry Rowen, eds, *The Silicon Valley Edge: A Habitat for Innovation and Entrepreneurship* (Stanford: Stanford University Press, 2000), 158–183. For a treatment of Shockley Semiconductor laboratory, see Michael Riordan and Lillian Hoddeson, *Crystal Fire: The Birth of the Information Age* (W. W. Norton Company: New York, 1997), 225–253. For the founders' conception of the market at the time of the firm's founding, see 'New Palo Alto Company Plans to Produce Transistors', *Palo Alto Daily Times*, October 17, 1957, collection of the author; Victor Grinich, oral history interview conducted by the author, February 7, 1996; Thomas Bay, oral history interview conducted by the author, July 2, 1996. For Fairchild Semiconductor policies regarding military research contracts, see Noyce, interview conducted by Herb Kleiman, Herb Kleiman collection, M827, Archives and Special Collections, Stanford University.

25 Gordon Moore, 'The Role of Fairchild in Silicon Technology in the Early Days of Silicon Valley', *Proceedings of the IEEE* 1998 (86: 1), 53–62; Jay Last, 'Meetings Reports etc. 10/57–3/59', courtesy of Jay Last. For machine shops in the Bay Area in the 1950s, see Arnold Wihtol, oral history interview conducted by the author, March 5, 1996 and Julius Blank, oral history interview conducted by the author, June 20, 1996.

26 For a treatment of the reliability of military avionics equipment in the mid-1950s, see James Bridges, 'Progress in Reliability of Military Electronics Equipment during 1956', *IRE Transactions for Reliability and Quality Control*, 11 (1957), 1–7; Anonymous, 'USAF Reliability Emphasis Grows', *Aviation Week*, April 1, 1957, 28.

27 Hoerni, 'Semiconductor Device', U.S. Patent 3064,167, filed May 1, 1959, granted November 13, 1962; Hoerni, 'Method of Manufacturing Semiconductor Devices', U.S. Patent 3,064,167, filed May 1, 1959, granted March 20, 1962; Hoerni, oral history interview conducted by the author, February 4, 1996; Noyce, 'Semiconductor Device-and-Lead Structure', U.S. Patent 2,981,877, filed July 30, 1959.

28 For a treatment of Autonetics' component reliability improvement programme, see H. S. Scheffler, 'The Minuteman High Reliability Component Parts Program: History and Legacy', Rockwell International Report C81–451/201, July 31, 1981, National Air and Space Museum.

29 Martin Kenney and Richard Florida, 'Venture Capital in Silicon Valley: Fueling New Firm Formation', in Martin Kenney, ed., *Understanding Silicon Valley: The Anatomy of an Entrepreneurial Region* (Stanford : Stanford University Press, 2000); Arthur Rock, 'Davis and Rock', July 13, 1961, courtesy of Jay Last.

30 For a treatment of McNamara's reform of the procurement process, see Fred Kaplan, *The Wizards of Armageddon* (New York, 1983); special issue devoted to McNamara's policies, *Missiles and Rockets*, volume 12, March 25, 1963; Robert Freund, *Competition and Innovation in the Transistor*

Industry, Ph.D. Dissertation, Department of Economics, Duke University, 1971, 44.

31 For a treatment of the impact of the Department of Defense's new procurement policies on component manufacturers, see Theodore Moreno, 'Government Pricing and Procurement Policies', *The Microwave Journal*, January 1963, 165–166.

32 For a treatment of Varian's diversification into the commercial market, see Timothy Lenoir and Lécuyer, 'Instrument Makers and Discipline Builders: The Case of NMR', *Perspectives on Science*, 4 (1995), 97–165.

33 Anonymous, 'All Transistor TV', *Leadwire*, Fall 1962, courtesy of Michael Brozda.

34 Lécuyer, 'Silicon for Industry: Component Design, Mass Production, and the Move to Commercial Markets at Fairchild Semiconductor, 1960–1967', *History and Technology*, 16 (1999), 179–216.

35 Ibid.

36 Charles Sporck, oral history interview conducted by the author, May 15, 1995; Bay, oral history interview conducted by the author, July 2, 1996; Moore, oral history interview conducted by the author and Ross Bassett, February 18, 1997.

37 Kenney and Florida, 'Venture Capital in Silicon Valley: Fueling New Firm Formation'.

38 Unlike Fairchild Semiconductor, its spin-offs did not set up independent research laboratories. Products were developed on the manufacturing line – which dispensed of the complex process of transfering products and processes from the research atory to the manufacturing plant.

39 William Eitel, 'Electronics Considered Pace-Setter in Region's Development', *Redwood City Tribune*, December 27, 1962, collection 64–94, San Mateo County Museum Historical Association, Redwood City.

40 Don Valentine, 'Sequoia Capital', in Udayan Gupta, *Done Deals: Venture Capitalists Tell Their Stories* (Boston: Harvard Business School Press, 2000), 165–178.

Chapter 4

Too many bends in the river

The decline of the Connecticut River Valley machine tool industry 1950–2002*

Robert Forrant

Introduction

The central question animating this article is: what happened to the US machine tool industry after the Second World War? In the first section, a brief description of the industry is provided, followed by a discussion of the rise and decline of an important machine tool and precision metalworking region, the Connecticut River Valley of Western New England, which stretches from the Atlantic Ocean in Southern Connecticut through Western Massachusetts and along the Vermont-New Hampshire border. The various strategies Japanese and US firms employed in their development of numerical control (NC) technologies are then assessed. A look at these efforts helps us to understand the US industry's precipitous decline after about 1970. The final section summarizes the problems faced by the US machine tool industry in the post-war period.

Background

For twenty years after the Second World War, the country's pre-eminence in machine tool design and manufacture, coupled with the productivity advantages that accrued to goods producers who utilized the machines, enabled tool builders and goods producers to prosper. Global prominence was aided by the fact that there was only minimal foreign competition for domestic machine tool sales to the automobile, aircraft, and other durable goods sectors. In such a virtuous circle of profitability US machine makers employed thousands of well-paid machinists. But in the late 1960s Japanese and German machine tool builders presented a concerted challenge for global market share and greater access to the extremely large US domestic market in particular.

The torpid response to this challenge resulted in staggering job losses in formerly prosperous machine tool regions as global market share slumped to under 7 per cent by 1990, from 25 per cent in 1965. The machine tool industry rode a 'death spiral' precipitated by heightened international competition and managerial deficiencies at home. In an astonishing role-reversal, the country became the world's largest importer of machine tools, while goods producers lost their early access to top-notch conventional and state-of-the-art machine tools, with the notable competitive advantages over foreign goods producers these machines once conveyed.

In 1981, sensing their historical dominance of the industry slipping away, the presidents of several US machine tool companies undertook a two-week fact-finding tour of Japan in the hope of gaining fresh insight into the industry's future. Arranged by National Machine Tool Builders Association (NMTBA), participants observed how tool-builders in Japan had increased their global market share. No 'magic bullet' explained Japan's precipitate advance to machine tool prominence, tour members realized.

> Nowhere in the thirteen factories toured by our study group did we see any unique manufacturing technology. In general Japanese machine tool builders use the same types of machinery to build their products as in America. However, the equipment and technology are very intelligently applied and many builders are investing heavily in the latest technology to improve productivity further.[1]

The US delegation learned that their Japanese counterparts placed a good deal of emphasis on collaborative research for the development of new products, spent a considerable portion of profits upgrading their capital equipment, and promoted shop-floor continuous improvement with all-round skills training. According to industry analyst Anthony DiFilippo, capital investments by US tool builders dropped after 1970 as Vietnam War orders dissipated. By 1980, these expenditures were lower, in inflation-adjusted dollars, than in 1965. Shortly after the NMTBA's Japan trip, a survey of forty-three US machine tool firms by the National Research Council (NRC) affirmed that 40 per cent of the equipment on factory floors was at least twenty years old, compared to 18 per cent in Japan. The NRC also discovered that many US firms had abandoned their apprenticeship programs. In other words, critical aspects of what US tool builders had determined were reasons for success among their Japanese rivals were being neglected at home.[2]

Industry overview

Generally speaking, the machine tool industry is a small but nonetheless essential sector of manufacturing. It accounts for approximately 2 per cent of manufacturing employment in developed countries. Machine tools are power-driven, cut or form metal, and are utilized in the manufacture of products or to make the machines on which goods are produced. Long-term collaborative relationships between final goods producers and machinery builders very often generate productivity-enhancing innovations that bolster firm, industry and national competitiveness. For example, at the opening of the twentieth century a series of machine tool technical advances proved instrumental to the evolution of the automobile assembly line. In William Corcoran's view, 'technological change within the machine tool industry translates into technological change in manufacturing processes themselves, yielding lower costs, higher quality, and new products'.[3]

There are several market segments in the industry, including low-cost basic machines like the drill press, computer-controlled machines, and expensive and complex computer-controlled multi-axis machining centres. Heavily-capitalized firms produce such things as customized multi-million dollar transfer lines for automobile manufacturers or pharmaceutical companies and machining centres for the aerospace industry. Small and typically family-owned enterprises build general-purpose machines such as lathes and milling machines that may cost as little as $10,000-$20,000. On the whole, firms concentrate on a particular product or fairly precise market segment. Important customers included the defence, aerospace, automotive, appliance, agricultural equipment, medical, and telecommunications industries.

Distinctions exist in how machines are controlled. Conventional machines, like the drill press, are operated by a worker who places the part to be machined in a fixture and manipulates a handle to bring a cutting tool in contact with the part. In the case of a numerically controlled (NC) drill press, the machine is guided by a computer programme most often written by an engineer. The cutting tool travels into the part as instructed by the program with little if any guidance by a worker. These machines are quite often set up to perform large quantity runs on a limited number of different parts. The operator will likely attend to several machines at once. Computer numerical control (CNC) automation permits operators, parts designers, and engineers to enter the dimensions and details for numerous highly intricate parts onto a computer linked to several machine tools. With numerous programmes stored in its memory, a CNC machine can perform highly complex work on parts of varying shapes and sizes throughout the work-day with little lost manufacturing time caused by setting and resetting the equipment for the various parts. Individual machines can also be programmed to work together to perform a series of machining operations on complex parts with very little, if any, worker handling involved.

Due to their productivity-enhancing capabilities and versatility, since the mid-1980s NC and CNC machines have replaced many conventional machines on factory floors. In 1976, the share of CNC grinding machines sold among all grinding machines was 1 per cent in the major tool-producing countries. By 1984, sales of such machines amounted to 11 per cent of market share and climbed to over 60 per cent of market share by 2000. As we shall see in the third section of this article, the US industry failed to capture a healthy share of the growing market for computer-controlled machines, and this contributed to the collapse of several venerable Connecticut River Valley machine tool builders.[4]

Adding to the industry's difficulties were merger waves in the late 1960s, the mid-1980s and the late–1990s which often 'resulted in the acquisition of machine tool firms by large, diversified companies that had not previously been in the machine tool business'. This was undeniably the case for numerous, once-independent firms in the Connecticut River Valley. When machine tool sales soared, their new owners invested the profits in other businesses, but during downturns the assets of their machine tool divisions were sold off to generate cash, thus weakening the tool builder when business returned.[5]

As the US industry restructured, what became of employment? Not surprisingly, thousands of highly skilled workers lost their jobs throughout the industrial Northeast and Midwest. In fact, between 1967 and 2000 employment declined from 120,000 to 44,000. The locus of market strength shifted as well. In 1998, fifty-six of the world's top two hundred machine tool firms by sales operated in Italy, 49 in Germany, and 25 in the US, and for most of the 1990s the four largest builders were Japanese. For 1999, Japan ($7.7B) and Germany ($7.5B) were the world's top producers. They accounted for close to half the world's output. Since 1982, Japan has remained the world's top producer on the strength of its dominance of the computer-controlled machinery market. Its machine tool trade surplus in 1999 was $4.9B, compared to Germany's surplus of $1.6B.

By comparison, in 1999 the US incurred the world's largest machine tool trade deficit, $2.8B.[6] Contributing to Japan's global market strength, Japan-based FANUC has been the world's largest producer of computer control systems, the brains of advanced machine tools for thirty years.[7]

Table 4.1 US machine tool employment in thousands 1975–1995

Year	Total Employment	Production Workers
1975	88.0	57.4
1977	88.5	57.3
1979	104.3	68.9
1981	104.4	67.3
1983	69.1	39.8
1985	73.0	45.7
1987	63.4	39.9
1989	67.3	43.6
1991	59.5	36.9
1993	51.4	31.4
1995	57.0	35.7

Source: Association for Manufacturing Technology, *Economic Handbook of the Machine Tool Industry* (McLean, VA, 1996).

Table 4.2 Ten largest machine tool builders in 1997 by sales (in millions of US dollars)

Company	Country	Sales
Yamazaki Mazak	Japan	1253.0
Amada	Japan	1214.3
FANUC	Japan	1007.4
Thyssen Maschinenbau	Germany	922.3
Okuma Machinery Works	Japan	873.5
Fuji Machine	Japan	815.4
UNOVA, Inc.	US	789.8
Trumpf Group	Germany	778.2
Mori Seki	Japan	740.7
Toyoda Machine Works	Japan	650.9

Source: Association For Manufacturing Technology, *1997 Machine Tool Scorecard* (McLean, VA, 1998).

Table 4.3 Global market share by percentage among the top three producers

	1964	1970	1975	1980	1985	1990	1996	1999
United States	25.1	18.5	17.3	18.1	12.6	6.7	12.6	12.8
Japan	6.4	14.2	7.8	14.4	24.8	23.2	23.6	23.0
Germany	15.9	18.9	17.6	17.8	14.8	18.9	20.1	21.0

Source: Association for Manufacturing Technology, *Economic Handbook of the Machine Tool Industry* (McLean, VA, 1996, 1999).

Springfield and the Connecticut River Valley: an early machine tool centre

Springfield, Massachusetts, is located at the approximate centre of a two hundred-mile industrial corridor along the Connecticut River between Bridgeport, Connecticut, and Windsor, Vermont. The river valley started securing its diverse manufacturing base soon after 1794, when Congress selected Springfield as the site for a federal armoury.[8] By the 1830s, the Armory functioned as the *de facto* hub of a flourishing district populated by inventive metalworking firms. Hundreds of skilled mechanics and machine designers took a stint at the Armory before traveling to other clusters of machine tool and metalworking companies throughout New England. Because of the diffusion of the Armory's innovative manufacturing techniques, for most of the nineteenth century the valley's goods producers enjoyed technological advantages over many other parts of the country. According to David Hounshell: 'The Armory acted both as a clearing house for technical information and a training ground for mechanics who later worked for private arms makers or for manufacturers of other goods'.[9]

During the 1840s, Windsor, Vermont (population 2,800), produced rifles, sewing machines, and machine tools in twenty metalworking firms. In 1860, on the eve of the Civil War, Springfield, Massachusetts, claimed seventy-three machine shops, six cotton factories, three paper mills, four printing concerns, two tool factories, a saw factory, several saw and grist mills, two brass foundries, two plough manufactories, and eight firms involved in the production of railroad cars and coaches. After the Civil War, the valley's machinery makers built specialized equipment for New England's pulp and paper and shoe industries, textile companies, watch-makers, furniture manufacturers, munitions makers, typewriter and bicycle builders, and jewelry makers. Soon after the turn of the century, firms in Springfield, Massachusetts, and Springfield, Vermont sold machinery to several fledgling automobile companies.[10]

Between 1885 and 1890, machinery output in Massachusetts rose a spectacular 158 per cent, and when the twentieth century opened the state's machinery builders ranked second in the nation in sales ($2.6M) behind Ohio ($6.4M). Connecticut ($1.8M) and Vermont ($284,000) ranked fourth and ninth, respectively. Twenty years later, New England's machine tool companies, the bulk of them in the Connecticut River valley, accounted for 40 per cent of national output, with Massachusetts and Connecticut ranked no less than third in total output for an array of machinery, including engine lathes, turret lathes, bench lathes, milling machines, grinding machines, boring machines, and planers.[11] Reciprocal relationships among tool builders, the hundreds of small, specialized tool-and-die shops and foundries that provided them with fixtures, tooling, gages, and made-to-order components, and final goods producers, enhanced the valley's competitiveness. Firms also benefited from the rich stock of skilled machinists and engineers living in what came to be known as 'precision valley'.[12]

Innovations spread among firms through the linked personal histories of many of the region's mechanics and engineers. For example, Pratt & Whitney Machine Tool began in 1869 under the direction of Francis Pratt and Amos Whitney. Prior to 1869, Pratt served his apprenticeship in the machine shop of a Lowell, Massachusetts, textile mill and Whitney served his at the Essex Machine Company in nearby Lawrence, where he built textile machinery. Coincidentally, they both moved to Hartford, Connecticut, in the late–1850s and worked in the toolroom of the Colt Firearms Company. Now friends, after a year at the Phoenix Iron Works in Hartford, they started their own company in 1869 building planers, spindle drills, gang drills, jig borers, thread millers, and surface grinders. Based on their gun-making experience, the two men established a gauge division at Pratt & Whitney to ensure the accuracy and the interchangeability of the parts being produced for their machine tools, as well as to guarantee, in turn, the accuracy of the parts their machines could turn out for their customers. Across the roof of the fast-growing Hartford plant, fifteen-foot-high letters spelled out the word ACCURACY, the firm's marketing credo.

Edward Bullard founded the Bullard Machine Tool Company in Bridgeport, Connecticut, in 1894. After completing an apprenticeship at the Whitin Machine Works in the late 1850s, Bullard worked in the toolroom at Colt Firearms and at Pratt & Whitney before opening his firm. Customers included Carnegie Steel, American Locomotive, National

Cash Register, Elgin Watch and Westinghouse. The company's sales breakthrough came in 1913, as the result of several months of collaboration between Bullard's son and engineers at the Ford Motor Company. The effort produced a multi-spindle drilling machine capable of machining an automobile flywheel in under two minutes, a feat that had previously taken eighteen minutes on a series of conventional machines. Further north, L. S. Starret's career began as an apprentice at the Athol Machine Works in Massachusetts. There, he received patents for a quick adjustable wrench and a combination square. Starret moved out on his own to make the wrench and the combination square and several additional machinists' tools, including thread gauges and the quick-adjusting micrometer.[13]

By the early twentieth century, 200 patents for such things as an automatic carding machine, an automatic screw machine, and a cross-feeding head had been issued to firms in central Vermont. Not to be outdone, in the opening decades of the twentieth century mechanics and engineers at Springfield, Massachusetts-based Stacy Machine Works invented an upright drill, the Bauch Machine Tool Company designed and built threading machines, and Hampden Grinding Wheel produced a new type of precision wheel.[14] Elsewhere, Moore Drop Forging's 1,400 foundry workers and machinists turned out machine beds for equipment going to the Mid-West's huge auto plants, Storms Drop Forge's 1,000 employees manufactured forgings for export world-wide, and the Perkins Gear and Machine Company's 350 pattern makers and skilled machinists crafted precision gears for global export.[15] Yet, these successes failed to stave off decline, for soon after the Second World War deep-seated structural weaknesses befell the industry and firms in Western New England's Connecticut River Valley suffered the ill-effects of the industry's stultification. The next section describes the downward post-war trajectory of three firms, Van Norman Company, Jones & Lamson, and Bryant Grinding. Their stories typify what happened among river valley tool builders.[16]

Van Norman

Hamilton, Ontario, brothers Charles E. and Fred D. Van Norman founded the Waltham Watch Tool Company in Watertown, Massachusetts, in 1888. Shortly, thereafter, the company was recruited to Springfield by the city's Board of Trade, in an effort to attract more skill-based industry to the region. It was incorporated as the Van Norman Machine Tool Company in 1890, and at start-up twenty-five workers produced bench lathes, moulding dies, and engravers' equipment. By 1910, its engineers had designed the first milling machines with adjustable cutter heads and the first cutter grinders. Customers purchased these machines in Greater-Springfield and in the Mid-West's growing auto industry.

Van Norman garnered its national reputation during the First World War, when it designed and built machines that produced industrial ball bearings. Until then, ball bearings had been largely imported from Germany, thus US war production would have been crippled without this engineering feat. The company grew in the inter-war years building equipment for the automotive industry and labour-saving, multi-purpose milling machines for the global market. Van Norman advertised its millers in the *American Machinist*, noting that the machines performed 'the work of many single-purpose machines' and cut operator idle time as much as 50 per cent 'because there is no waiting for specific machines' and no 'continual changing of the workpiece'.[17]

Turning a handsome profit, in the early1950s, Van Norman purchased several other Massachusetts machine tool firms to gain complementary product lines. Enlarged in this way, the company caught the attention of New York industrialist Herbert Segal, and in 1956 he acquired a 35 per cent controlling interest in company stock from the original owners' descendants. Springfield-area directors were replaced, and the company's headquarters was moved to New York City, where the offices for Segal's other holdings were located. Van Norman Machine Tools was now one of eight divisions in Van Norman Industries (VNI), a conglomerate with factories in California, Michigan, New Hampshire, Ohio, and Pennsylvania, and $50 million in annual sales.[18]

When he purchased Van Norman Machine, Segal had envisaged it becoming the centrepiece of what he referred to as the 'General Motors of the machine tool industry'. Plans for the construction of a Springfield factory to house VNI's entire machine tool division were announced in March 1957. But by late spring 1957, with the national economy slumping, machine tool orders fell as manufacturers curtailed capital equipment purchases. One hundred Van Norman workers lost their jobs, and the remainder of the workforce was employed only thirty-two hours a week. At year's end corporate sales were $47M, down from $49.8M the previous year. With corporate-wide profits a meagre $722,611, the machine tool division stagnated and the new plant was scrapped.

At the start of 1958, a group of Chicago investors provided VNI with a much-needed cash infusion by purchasing 100,000 company shares. The Chicago group assumed three seats on the fifteen-person board of directors and led cost-cutting efforts: corporate officers and supervisors were forced to absorb 5 per cent pay cuts; Segal's compensation was reduced by 10 per cent; and annual fees paid to corporate directors were cut in half to $2,000.[19] More layoffs and work-week reductions followed and rumors circulated that VNI was going to discontinue production in the city. Demise seemed imminent when in November 1958 the sixty-four year old Segal announced his retirement. Van Norman had not become the 'General Motors of the machine tool industry'. When Segal left, only 350 workers laboured in the machine tool division, an astonishing drop from the 1,500 workers in place in 1956 when he took over.[20]

Despite mounting losses, hope was rekindled when Charles Meyers, president of the Morse Twist Drill and Machine Company – a cutting tool division of VNI – replaced Segal. When the economy accelerated at the end of 1960, Meyers invested in the production of several new machines, including an NC grinder, an NC machine for miniature ball bearing manufacture for the missile, aircraft, and medical instruments industries, and a multi-axis drilling machine.[21] These new machines resulted from Meyers' Integrated Design Program, whereby VNI's customers were surveyed regarding their future manufacturing requirements. However, when a member of the Chicago investors group became vice-president for finance there ensued an internal struggle for the corporation's still meagre profits and the promising programme was jettisoned well before anyone could seriously judge the long-term potential for providing the firm with an expanded customer base.[22] Without the promise of new work that the Integrated Design Program so tantalizingly offered, by the end of 1963 half of the factory's 500 workers were on a 35-hour week and every worker feared for their future.

VNI merged with the Universal American Corporation in 1962 and five years later it was acquired by the Gulf & Western Corporation. Under Gulf & Western, employment skidded under 300, its lowest level in over thirty years. The factory limped into the 1970s, when in the fourth ownership change in twenty years it became an appendage of Minnesota-based Winona Tool Manufacturing. It soon became apparent that Winona had purchased the plant simply and cynically for its globally-recognized reputation, not for its skills and production capacity. The factory stayed open only four more years. While employment was phased out, a skeleton crew of workers expended their last days performing a task that must have rankled; they affixed the Van Norman Machine Tool name-plate on Italian machine tools being imported by Winona for North American distribution.[23]

Jones & Lamson

In 1920, fifty firms and 4,000 workers in Central Vermont crafted machine tools, fixtures, and specialized parts for final goods producers across the US. At the conclusion of the Second World War, 8,000 machinists plied their craft in central Vermont. The 'big three' machine tool firms – Jones & Lamson (J&L), Fellows Gear Shaper, and Bryant Grinding – employed 817, 530, and 229 workers, respectively, in 1939; in 1941 an intense war-time production schedule hiked employment to 2,220 at J&L, 1,584 at Fellows, and 861 at Bryant. From 1941 to 1945, they shipped over 12,000 machines. Without an increase in worker housing, many machinists spent the harsh Vermont winters living in canvas tents pitched on relatively flat land near the railroad lines that hauled new machine tools to aircraft and tank factories across the US.[24]

Started in Windsor in 1824 as the Connecticut River Company, after several permutations the custom gun shop Robbins & Lawrence was formed in 1849. Open under that name until 1856, the company benefited from lucrative federal contracts for rifles before and during the Civil War. To complete these contracts on time, the company's skilled mechanics devised their own production machinery, and over time machine-making became the company's core business. Reincorporated in 1879 as the Jones & Lamson Machine Company, the firm relocated to Springfield, Vermont in 1888. There the company produced the country's first flat-turret lathes. Other innovative products followed, including an optical comparator in 1919 and a thread-grinding machine in 1920. J&L's workforce peaked at slightly over 3,000 in late 1944, with workers on gruelling twelve-hour shifts for six days a week.

Soon after the Second World War, J&L's founding families relinquished day-to-day control of the company and it was acquired outright by Textron in the late 1960s. At the time, Textron also purchased Connecticut-based Bridgeport Machines and Bryant Grinding, J&L's near neighbour. Indeed, from the late–1960s to early–1980s conglomerates like Textron purchased several US machine tool companies. In paroxysms of hubris, the managers of conglomerates felt that their central engineering staffs and corporate level R&D could overcome what they felt were the industry's weaknesses.

Textron sold J&L in 1984 to a financial holding group. Prior to the sale, production managers with over one hundred years of collective machine tool production knowledge were dismissed, to be replaced by Textron's management team. While the new team may have known how to manufacture something, then J&L quality manager Faye Kingsbury recalled that it was not machine tools. Workers 'laughed at their new managers and wondered what the hell they were trying to do', he recalled. Textron's top management located their offices in a non-machine tool plant over 125 miles away in Connecticut. For Jim Halvorsen, a long-time manager at nearby Bryant, 'having no strong local operations manager contributed mightily to product line decline at J&L in the 1970s'. Unable to boost sales, in 1986 J&L filed for bankruptcy protection. It was purchased by The Goldman Group in 1988.

In describing Textron's takeover of J&L and Bridgeport Machine in Connecticut, Arthur Alexander concluded that profits from its machine tool division were regularly diverted to other business activities rather than to enhance the machine tool business. 'Over a decade-long continuation of this policy, these two Textron divisions lacked new lines of competitive products, especially in numerical control'.[25] The irony here is that J&L brought out a basic low-cost computer-controlled lathe in the late–1960s and its order book quickly filled up. However, scant investments were made in figuring out how this burgeoning demand could be satisfied. Assuming that they absolutely controlled the US domestic market, J&L informed far too many potential buyers to expect a one-year wait for machines. Kingsbury believed that this cavalier attitude toward customers was understandable in the 1950s and early–1960s, when even conventional lathes from Japan suffered numerous design and mechanical flaws. However, at a 1971 international tool show in Los Angeles, Kingsbury viewed Japanese lathes that were 'foolproof for accuracy', were cheaper than J&L's lathes, and, most importantly, could be delivered on time.

Max Holland uncovered a similar situation at New Hampshire-based Burgmaster. When the company introduced its first series of NC lathes in 1964, orders doubled to $16.4M for the machines in one year, yet shipments increased only 18 per cent. By January 1966, Burgmaster had a $30 million backlog for its lathes, yet it was shipping $900,000 worth of machines monthly.[26] Japanese firms, eager to fill the vacuum created by the failures of companies like J&L, produced basic lathes and simple NC lathes in sufficient quantity to meet US customer demand by the early 1970s. How this came about is discussed in greater detail in the next section of this article.

During a 2001 interview, a still-incredulous Halvorsen described one firm that proudly proclaimed that it built its lathes on a 'different size-a-month' schedule. A customer placing an order in February for the type of machine produced during January politely was informed that a one-year wait was likely for the desired machine to be built again!

Burgmaster and J&L were abandoned by hundreds of disgruntled customers because of the even more profound abandonment of Burgmaster and J&L by their corporate owners' refusal to invest in the expanded manufacturing capacity and shop-floor improvements needed to grow market share and, at the very least, preserve existing jobs.[27]

Bryant Grinding

Bryant Grinding opened its doors in the early – 1900s. William Bryant, who had studied engineering at the University of Vermont, received a patent for a revolutionary grinding machine, and it became the company's core business. The machine made it possible for a worker to grind both the internal and outer surfaces of a part without it having to be repositioned or placed in a second machine. This saved precious set-up time and, equally important, because the part was located just once in the machine, the finished part's quality improved a great deal. Like J&L, Bryant prospered during the Second World War. For example, it shipped 1300 machines in January 1943, compared to 329 in January 1940.

For a time, Bryant dodged the problems attendant with buy-outs already vexing its Vermont neighbour. For example, when in 1958 it became a subsidiary of the diversified machine tool manufacturer Ex-Cell-O, local management remained intact. However, Textron's purchase disrupted Bryant's management structure and the company began to drift. Orders dropped in the early 1980s, as European countries protected their domestic markets. Furthermore, buoyed by successes in several basic machine tool markets, Japanese firms now produced computer-controlled grinding machines in a direct challenge for Bryant's lucrative US car builders' market. According to Halvorsen, when auto production 'went global we lost important engineering relationships with our customers and now foreign proximity built some business for European competitors'. Bryant's executives, including Halvorsen, believed that it would take at least ten years for Japanese companies to build computer-controlled machines equal to Bryant's. However, just as Faye Kingsbury's assumptions were proven false, Halvorsen was chastened when he viewed an exhibit of extremely well-built Japanese NC grinding machines at a 1983 international tool show in Hanover, Germany. He recalled thinking the world 'no longer needs the US machine tool industry'.[28]

For a few years, Bryant preserved a semblance of its markets by providing excellent customer service. Technicians accompanied all new machines to set them up and guarantee performance on their customers' shop floors. But 'when the financial world fully took control of the manufacturing world in the mid 1980s this customer-builder link was deemed too costly by Textron's accountants', according to Halvorsen. Across the country, Bryant's field technicians and engineers were fired and after-sales customer service scaled back. After alienating its once-secure customer base, Bryant's market for high-end grinders slipped. A series of debilitating mergers, acquisitions and flirtations with bankruptcy culminated in the company's 1990 purchase by the Goldman Industrial Group, a financial holding company. At the time, Goldman also took control of Bryant's Vermont neighbours, Fellows Corporation and J&L.[29]

Alternative trajectories: numerical control in the US and Japan

Significant differences exist in the development of numerical control technologies in Japan and the US, and these differences help to clarify why the US industry lost so much market share in the 1970s and 1980s. With their government's technical and financial support, Japanese firms collaborated in the development of the low-cost, basic NC machinery. A single company, FANUC, focused on the development of machinery controls and software to establish an industry standard. These machines provided Japanese machine tool builders with an entry point into the US market.[30] By comparison, a dozen US builders constructed expensive, specialized NC machines mainly for defence contractors, often with their own brand of controls. No effort to establish an industry-wide standard for controls gained favour. The result was that FANUC's 'controls became the *de facto* world standard, with an estimated 70% of the global market, providing Japanese machine-tool makers with a substantial first-mover advantage'.[31]

US industry leaders were cognizant of ongoing efforts in Japan to develop NC equipment. In 1959, the trade publication *American Machinist* dutifully reported that Japanese firms were 'moving into the international arena big time'. However, it pejoratively concluded that Japanese machinery was nondescript and appealed simply to 'Southeast Asian and other industrially backward nations'. *American Machinist* also noted that Japan's Ministry of International Trade and Industry (MITI) championed research on a numerically-controlled jig borer suitable for use in small shops. However, there is no evidence that the industry's leaders ever fully grasped the long-term market threat posed by these activities.[32]

Ironically, NC technology's roots were in research at the Servo-mechanisms Laboratory at the Massachusetts Institute of Technology (MIT). MIT's involvement came via a subcontract from machine tool builder John Parsons. Eventually, MIT garnered a contract from the Air Force, jettisoned Parsons, and in 1952 it demonstrated its own control system on a Cincinnati Machine Tool vertical milling machine. Backed by the US Air Force, using MIT's engineering expertise Cincinnati Milling, Bendix, Kearney & Trecker, and Giddings & Lewis, individually partnered with aircraft builders to produce NC machines. Five companies – Bendix Aviation, Cincinnati Milling, General Electric, Giddings & Lewis, and Electronic Control Systems – began designing machinery controls. Eventually, the NC divisions of these companies marketed their controllers, but with only limited success.[33] In addition, thirty-one smaller firms rushed development of control systems applicable for basic machine tools. These controls carried exotic names like 'Electrolimit', 'Digitork System', 'Inductosym', 'Autopilot' and 'Weditrol Positioning'. Prices ranged from $110,000 for a jig borer with controls, to under $10,000 for basic controls matched to a simple machine like a drill press or small lathe. No collaboration between these smaller firms and the MIT project materialized.[34]

The US Air Force directed the work of Cincinnati Milling, Bendix, Kearney & Trecker and Giddings & Lewis through its considerable investment in the MIT project. The resultant US Air Force-MIT machines worked well in a controlled laboratory environment, but when the machines were placed on actual shop floors and became exposed to vibrations, electrical interference, dirt, and untrained operators, this changed. Furthermore, because the firms building the prototypes were heavily subsidized by the government, they paid little attention to costs. Too specialized, too fragile, and too costly, no broad-based market emerged for the machines. Instead, the US Air Force purchased and gave away 100 five-axis continuous-path profile milling machines, twenty-five each built by Cincinnati Milling, Giddings & Lewis, Kearney & Trecker and Morey Machine.

In the US, the research and development of NC machine tools became convoluted, because too many firms were involved in a thoroughly uncoordinated way, the all-important controls were developed without uniform standards, and the machine tools and the controls were too often built to engage in exotic and difficult tasks with minimal application to the broader customer base. This was a far cry from the collaborative culture found in the nineteenth century in Connecticut River Valley and other centres of machine tool innovation.[35] According to Anderson Ashburn: 'A common expression among people involved in the early years of NC was that it had developed from the roof instead of from the foundation'.[36] The machines that were built in the US were, according to

Holland, 'far more sophisticated than anything a civilian manufacturer might need, or be willing to pay for'.[37]

In sharp relief to the helter-skelter approach in the US, controls were built in Japan by Fujitsu Automatic Numerical Controls (FANUC) in a more 'Armory-like' collaborative endeavor with tool builders, and these controls quickly became the globally-recognized standard.[38] Japan's MITI and the Japan Machine Tool Builders' Association (JMTBA) formulated a comprehensive strategy to rebuild the country's manufacturing base. The JMTBA was formed in 1952 by forty of the country's largest builders. It acted as their members' voice with the government, and facilitated the exchange of technical information between firms.

Two national laws, the *Gaishi-ho* (Foreign Capital Law, 1950), and the *Kikaikogyo Rinji Sochio-ho* (Temporary Measures for the Development of the Machinery Industry Law, 1956) helped machine tool builders gain access to capital and foreign technology. MITI brokered 29 licensing agreements with foreign machine makers between 1961 and 1964, while it discouraged direct foreign investment in Japanese machine tool firms.[39] The licensing helped US firms gain limited entry to Japan, but over time such agreements cut into sales there. Machinery exports to Japan fell 50% in 1963 and another 50% in 1965; by comparison, Japan's exports to the US skyrocketed from $2.4 million in 1964 to $26.2 million in 1967, and they climbed steadily thereafter. By the early 1970s, MITI advocated that 50% of Japan's machine tool industry output should be NC equipment. Machinery makers were 'encouraged in the development of NC machine tools which would be useful to the typical small Japanese manufacturer that was becoming increasingly interested in automation'.[40]

Japanese firms collaborated on research and development of NC technologies with the encouragement and financial support of the government. While FANUC developed controls and software, tool-builders worked on machinery design and improved manufacturing techniques. Second, since the fusion of traditional machine tools with new technologies was complex, the industry 'did not aim for high-performance niches, but for consistent, reliable low-cost, standard products that many firms could use'.[41] In other words, it started at the foundation and only after organizational learning increased were more complex designs attempted.

Japan's efforts were exhibited at the 1970 international machine tool convention in Osaka, Japan. On display was a system of twenty-eight linked machine tools operated with FANUC controls.[42] Four years later in *World Manufacturing*, Tokyo Bureau chief Michael Mealey reported that the entire production process at FANUC's Hino factory was under computer control. 'Computers keep track of orders, parts inventory, parts purchase, production schedules, and parts testing', he wrote. In 1975, FANUC opened a service centre in the US to boost exports and the rout of US builders was on. By the mid 1980s, FANUC had 40% to 50% of the control market worldwide, and Siemens, General Electric, and General Motors entered joint ventures with FANUC to maintain a presence in the controls market.[43]

The Valley grinds down

What remains of the machine tool industry and related precision metalworking in the Connecticut River Valley at the start of the twenty-first century? Tool builders and final goods producers went through a tortuous decline in the 1970s and 1980s, punctuated with plant closings and the loss of thousands of jobs. The valley's long-standing reputation as a centre for innovation now badly tarnished, the 'ACCURACY' sign atop the Pratt & Whitney Machine Tool building became a distant memory for the thousands of people who had once toiled there. How far was the fall? In 1954, Connecticut had 119,000 workers in skilled metalworking occupations; by the early – 1970s there were 102,000 workers so employed; and in 1982 approximately 95,000. Massachusetts factories employed 241,816 such workers in 1954 and 150,000 in 1982. The greatest collapse occurred in Central Vermont, where about 1000 machinists were employed in the early 1980s, down from well over 10,000 machinists in 1947.

Up and down the River Valley, research and development was constricted in the small firms, and when larger tool builders were subsumed by conglomerates, out-of-touch top management halted investments in their machine tool divisions.[44] In his 1966 history of the machine tool industry, Harless Wagoner offered a prescient critique of the industry's lack of ongoing investment. In particular, he explained how this could hurt national productivity:

> The machine tool industry or, at least, particular firms in the industry deserve full credit for having greatly improved machine tool capacity and performance on a wide range of machining problems. This is true even though it is believed that greater technical progress could have been made had the industry devoted greater effort to research and development and had been given greater support in these efforts by machine tool users, and the federal government. It also appears, however, that as machine tool builders became more preoccupied with business problems, cost accounting, statistics, controlling price

competition, profit ratios, reserves, etc., they devoted less attention to purely technical problems.[45]

Echoing Wagoner, Anderson Ashburn concluded that since about 1970 the management of most machine tool companies in the United States shifted into the hands of people with financial rather than technical backgrounds. Overall, the industry failed to invest enough in itself, relying instead on Department of Defense prime contractors and the manufacturers of computers and controllers to spur innovation.[46] Far more adept at the timely manufacture of affordable NC equipment, Japanese builders gobbled up the escalating US demand for these machines. In the 1980s, basic CNC lathes and highly versatile machining centres made up 30% of world-wide sales and the bulk of US orders was filled by imports. Table 4.4 shows the rapid rise in imports between 1980 and 1986. Thus, the domestic market slipped and regions like the Connecticut River Valley lost their luster.[47]

Even when innovation took place, such as Van Norman's collaborative customer-builder design program, efforts were short-circuited by the financial constraints of conglomerate ownership. Ashburn, citing a 1985 study by the Technical Change Centre of London, summarizes this failure:

> both European and US firms seemed to view investment in improving productivity as an exercise in short-run cost reduction for new products. In contrast, the Japanese firms viewed manufacturing engineering in a much more fundamental way, considering such investment as an important element in product design and development and a major long-run source of international competitiveness.[48]

Table 4.4 Numerically controlled metal-cutting machine tools produced and consumed in the US, 1980–86

	Domestic Production	Export	Import	Consumption
1980	8,889	959	4,524	12,454
1982	5,116	659	5,549	10,006
1984	5,124	479	7,655	12,300
1986	4,633	606	12,146	16,173

Source: Ashburn, 'The Machine Tool Industry', 1990, p. 53.

According to Kingsbury and Halvorsen, even with the domestic market shrinking, US builders eschewed exports. In a fit of myopia, they wrongly assumed that the home market was still their own. The failure to market globally during these years was 'a major problem', because the primary locus of consumption 'had moved away from the United States to Europe and the Pacific Rim. Exports were vital to industry growth'.[49]

Into the 1980s, US builders did not sell large numbers of computer-controlled machines in either the domestic or the foreign market.[50] The National Research Council determined that

> The traditional practice of order backlog management, which served US machine tool builders well for several decades, was based on an implicit assumption that potential foreign competitors did not have the resources to take advantage of wide swings in the US tool market. Whether this assumption was ever valid, it certainly was not so by the late 1970s. By that time many foreign firms had the resources to offer fast delivery of quality machines to US customers who did not wish to wait for backlogs to be worked down by their domestic suppliers.[51]

Japan's NC design-and-build path established a domestic market which became the springboard for global success. Between 1970 and 1974, small to medium-size firms made up from one-third to one-half the market for numerically controlled machine tools in Japan.[52] Computer-controlled machine tools comprised 9% of unit output in Japan and 2% in the United States in 1979; output figures were 42% and 7% respectively in 1991. The adjusted market value of all NC machines shipped by US builders in 1991 sank below 1982 levels, even as over these years domestic demand soared to $2.2 billion in 1991, from $1.25 billion in 1983.[53]

In the summary of their 1981 trip to Japan, US builders noted that 'Every Japanese machine tool builder's goal is market share and output volume, as opposed to profit. They will boldly sacrifice profits for several years to build the groundwork for later success'. Japanese firms succeeded because of the 'willingness of management to invest heavily in its future, market its products aggressively throughout the world, work doggedly toward long-term goals, and pay an unusual amount of attention to the training and motivation of its workforce'.[54] Merger waves had curtailed spending, and as one builder noted, conglomerates had no commitment to the industry and 'thought that they could make money by selling the same old designs and building them on depreciated equipment'.[55]

Leading US builders focused their post-war research and development efforts on Pentagon-size problems lured by the vision of large payoffs and lucrative cost-plus contracts. In one classic case, the government ordered the manufacture of 11 four-spindle, five-axis machines at a cost of $1 million each, when an existing four-axis machine costing $150,000 was already available. This insistence on customized machines raised design-and-build costs without affecting performance, and it deterred firms from designing machines with applications for their non-defence customers.[56]

Japan's market developments and enterprise finance strategies were augmented with training that promoted maximum shop-floor participation from machinists. The US travellers noted that

> Keeping their workplaces and machines in good order is a responsibility assigned to the operators themselves, along with maintaining output, helping fellow-workers and assuring they every part produced meets or exceeds quality standards. . . . each worker is trained to correct the minor problems that often arise in the course of the day, to conduct regular preventive maintenance to monitor and adjust equipment, and to search continually for ways to eliminate potential disruptions and improve efficiency.[57]

By comparison, the Van Norman, J&L, Bryant and Burgmaster histories show that conglomerate ownership eroded shop-floor skills and managerial talent. In a 1945 Pratt & Whitney catalogue is the following statement:

> It is not uncommon at P&W for succeeding generations of families to work here – grandfather, father, son – each passing on his skill and knowledge to the next in true New England fashion. The result has been a unique combination of hereditary craftsmanship with modern research that is reflected in everything we make.

The chain of so-called hereditary craftsmanship was broken, as were direct relationships with customers. J&L no longer had an onsite operations' manager after its purchase by Textron. Bryant severed it links with its customer base by firing service representatives. Burgmaster's machinists and engineers were no longer involved in reorganization efforts, and numerous shop-floor reorganization campaigns failed. Houdaille's acquisition of Burgmaster changed the plant from one based on knowledge and ability to one built on allegiance to the corporate way of doing things.

The 1994 Rand study of the industry concluded that US rivals used their factories 'as test beds for the latest tools, relying on workers to come up with new incremental improvements in products or the process of making them. This includes not only engineers, but production workers as well'. US managers pursued a 'lower skill strategy', unlike their international competitors in Germany and Japan, and this discouraged 'the most able young people from entering metalworking'. Firms terminated apprenticeship programmes, partially in response to the cyclical nature of the business; if managers were going to survive the industry's vagaries through massive layoffs, why invest in the workforce? Skill and historical knowledge became expendable, innovation's underpinnings were sheared off, and the industry's post-war trajectory remained negative.[58]

Coda

Vermont's Fellows, Bryant, and J&L had been purchased by The Goldman Industrial Group during the late 1980s and the early 1990s. For most of the 1990s, the United Electrical, Radio & Machine Workers Union, which represented workers in the Vermont plants, charged that Goldman was not reinvesting in the companies. In 1999 and 2000, workers publicly protested that no new machinery had been bought since Goldman took over. During a bitter round of negotiations in 2000 over the possible closing of Bryant, Goldman's negotiators admitted that this was true. Goldman's ownership, unionists charged, would result in 'the slow destruction' of the Vermont factories. At the start of 2001, fewer than 400 workers were employed in the three Vermont firms. In February 2002, Goldman filed for bankruptcy in US Bankruptcy Court, and machinery production ceased in central Vermont after 170 years. Goldman owed its employee pension fund nearly $8 million and had failed to make its required payments into the plan, thus prompting the federal Pension Benefit Guarantee Corporation – which guarantees payment of basic pension benefits for workers – to place liens on the Goldman-owned factories. The bankruptcy filing and production cessation followed.[59]

Robert Forrant postscript

Machinery building and precision metalworking prospered in the Merrimack River Valley from the late nineteenth century through the early 1960s, long after textile and apparel cities in New England ceased their economic growth. However, such firms could not escape a similar fate, and over half of Greater Springfield's manufacturing facilities closed between 1950 and 2000, with thousands of jobs lost. In *Beyond the Ruins: The Meanings of Deindustrialization*, Joseph Heathcott and Jefferson Cowie point out that

> Deindustrialization is not a story of a single emblematic place . . . or a specific time period, such as the 1980s; it was a much broader, more fundamental, historical transformation. What was labeled deindustrialization in the intense political heat of the late 1970s and early 1980s turned out to be a more socially complicated, historically deep, geographically diverse, and politically perplexing phenomenon than previously thought.

Such widespread economic dislocation in part explains how a drift rightwards took place in working-class voter behaviour in the early twenty-first century.

Notes

* Many thanks to Philip Scranton and John Wilson for extremely helpful comments and suggestions on how to improve this article. Of course, remaining errors and confusions are my own.

1 National Machine Tool Builders Association (NMTBA), *Meeting the Japanese Challenge* (McLean, VA, 1981), p. 5. On the trip were top managers of leading US builders, including Cross & Trecker, Giddings & Lewis, and Bridgeport Machines. Firms visited included Toyoda Machine Works, Mori Seiki and Fujitsu Fanuc.

2 Anthony DiFilippo, *Military Spending and Industrial Decline: A Study of the American Machine Tool Industry* (New York, 1986). National Research Council (NRC), *The US Machine Tool Industry and the Defense Industrial Base* (Washington, DC: 1983), p. 2. For a discussion of the centrality of links between indigenous innovation and national competitiveness, see Qiwen Lu and William Mass, 'Technology Transfer and Indigenous Innovation in Pre-Revolution China: Mechanical Engineering Capabilities and Textile Machinery Enterprises', *Journal of Industrial History*, 2 (1999), pp. 23–49.

3 William Corcoran, 'The Machine Tool Industry Under Fire', in Donald Losman and Shu-Jan Liang, eds, *The Promise of American Industry: An Alternative Assessment of Problems and Prospects* (New York, 1990), pp. 227–247, 227. In his history of the Burgmaster Company, Max Holland describes machine tools as the *mother* or *master* machines that make all other machines. Metal-cutting machines – including grinding machines, drilling machines, millers and lathes – account for approximately two-thirds of world output. Forming machines include presses to stamp metal into various shapes, metal shears and saws. The easiest way to distinguish between the two categories of metalworking equipment is to remember that

cutting machines remove material in the form of metal chips, while forming machines alter the shape of the material. A related sector designs and builds specialized dies, moulds, tooling, and fixtures for machine tool builders and other manufacturers, usually on a contract basis. For useful general histories of the industry see Joseph Wickham Roe, *English and American Tool Builders* (New York, 1926); John Glover and William Cornell, *The Development of American Industries* (New York, 1941), esp. ch. 26, 'The Machine Tool Industry': 557–76; L. T. Rolt, *A Short History of Machine Tools* (Cambridge, 1965); David Hounshell, *From the American System to Mass Production, 1830–1932: The Development of Manufacturing Technology in the United States* (Baltimore, 1984); Max Holland, *When the Machine Stopped: A Cautionary Tale from Industrial America* (Boston, 1989).

4 See Robert Forrant, 'The Global Machine Tool Industry', in Malcolm Warner, ed., *International Encyclopedia of Business and Management* (London, 2002), pp. 2309–2316; Critical Technologies Institute (CTI), *The Decline of the US Machine Tool Industry and Prospects for Sustainable Recovery* (Santa Monica, 1994) esp. 7–8.

5 M. Holland, *When the Machine Stopped*, p. 84. For example Bendix acquired the Warner & Swasey Company in 1983 and transferred most of Warner and Swasey's production to the Japanese company Murata, thus hollowing out this venerable company (NRC, *The US Machine Tool Industry*, 44).

6 Association for Manufacturing Technology (AMT), *The Economic Handbook of the Machine Tool Industry* (McLean, VA, 1995, 1999).

7 DiFilippo, *Military Spending and Industrial Decline*, p. 7; CTI, *The Decline of the US Machine Tool Industry*, vol. 1, pp. 11–12; AMT, *The Economic Handbook*; M. Tsuji, M, Ishikawa and M. Ishikawa, *Technology Transfer and Management in East Asian Machine Tool Industries* (Osaka, 1996), esp. pp. 31–5.

8 Michael Frisch, *Town into City: Springfield, Massachusetts and the Meaning of Community: 1840–1860* (Cambridge, MA, 1972). The Armory was described by one British visitor as 'beautifully situated on an eminence overlooking the town', see Nathan Rosenberg, ed., *The American System of Manufactures: The Report of the Committee on the Machinery of the United States 1855 and the Special Reports of George Wallis and Joseph Whitworth* (Edinburgh, 1969), p. 364. For a historical analysis of industrial growth in pre-Civil War New England see François Weil, 'Capitalism and Industrialization in New England, 1815–1845', *The Journal of American History* 84 (1998), pp. 1334–54. For a historical overview of the British industry in the late nineteenth and early twentieth centuries see A. J. Arnold, 'Innovation, deskilling and profitability in the British machine-tools industry: Albert Herbert 1887–1927', *Journal of Industrial History*, 2 (1999), pp. 50–71.

9 Hounshell, *From the American System*.

10 Hounshell, *From the American System*, pp. 33–4, 44. For Hounshell, the keys to Armory success were an early reliance on private arms contractors as a source for innovation and the perfecting of ways to inspect parts. Hounshell cites Felicia Deyrup's *Arms Makers of the Connecticut Valley* (Northampton, MA, 1948) for her documentation of instances when the Armory's pattern-makers and skilled foundry workers produced casting for area machine tool builders without the internal capacity to do so. For Vermont, Arthur F. Stone, *The Vermont of Today* (New York, 1929), esp. ch. 23.

11 Connecticut increased its share of the machine tool industry from 10.8% to 13.7% and Vermont's share increased from 1.7% to 6%. Massachusetts' share declined from 16% in 1900 to 7.0% in 1954. Harless Wagoner, *The US Machine Tool Industry from 1900–1950* (Cambridge, MA, 1966), p. 45.

12 The *Fourteenth United States Census* (1920) reported that 25% of the nation's machine tools were shipped from Massachusetts, Connecticut, and Rhode Island and that 20% of the country's machine tool firms employing more than 100 workers were located along the Connecticut River. Roe's *English and American Toolbuilders* contains numerous genealogies of firms that reveal the movement of key personnel from plant-to-plant in the Connecticut River Valley. Deyrup uncovered a contracting system that promoted a 'spirit of cooperation and mutual aid' which had much to do 'with the rapid development of the industry in the first thirty years of the nineteenth century' *Arms Makers*, p. 66. Frisch, *Town into City*, p. 15; M. Van Hosen Taber, *A History of the Cutlery Industry in the Connecticut Valley* (Northampton, MA, 1955).

13 For Pratt & Whitney's early history, R. F. V. Stanton, *Accuracy For Seventy Years 1860–1930* (Hartford, CT, 1930); for Bullard, Irwin Robinson, *Yankee Toolmaker* (Bridgeport, CT, 1955); and for Starret, Kenneth Cope, *Makers of American Machinist's Tools* (Mendham, NJ, 1994), pp. 73–112.

14 In 1910, of the 743 firms in the US producing automobiles, auto bodies, and parts, 100 were in Connecticut, Massachusetts, and Vermont, the majority in the river valley. By comparison, 113 such firms were in Michigan. *Thirteenth Census of the United States Vol. 10, Manufacturers* (Washington, DC, 1913). Commonwealth of Massachusetts, *A Directory of Massachusetts Manufacturers* (Boston, MA, 1913).

15 *Fourteenth Census of the United States Vol. 10* (Washington, DC, 1923); Robert Forrant, 'Neither a Sleepy Village Nor a Coarse Factory Town', *Journal of Industrial History* 4 (2001), pp. 24–47; Orra Stone, *History of Massachusetts Industries: Their Inception, Growth, and Success* (Boston, 1930), p. 539.

16 Robert Forrant, *Metalworking Plant Closings*.

17 *American Machinist* 90 (31 January 1946), p. 12; Robert Forrant, 'Neither a Sleepy Village'.

18 Larry Gormally, 'Van Norman: A Jewel of a Company', *Springfield Journal* 15, no. 14 (1990), pp. 4–5; Amy Glasmeier, *Manufacturing Time: Global Competition in the Watch Industry, 1795–2000* (New York, 2000), esp. ch. 3; *Springfield Morning Union* (SMU), 1 March 1957, 1, 28; 30 March 1957, 1.

19 *SMU*, 4 December 1957, 6; 2 February 1958, 1.

20 On deindustrialization in Springfield see Robert Forrant, 'The Roots of Connecticut River Valley Deindustrialization: The Springfield American Bosch Plant 1940–1975', *Historical Journal of Massachusetts* (forthcoming Winter 2003).

21 *SMU*, 26 April 1958, 13; 22 July 1958, 1; 18 August 1958, 1, 31; 13 November 1958, 1.

22 *SMU*, 7 April 1960, 1; 5 May 1960, 16; 18 June 1960, 11; 10 December 1960, 33; 3 August 1961, 2; 14 November 1961, 7. The machine cut the groove in the inner ring of the ballbearing to tolerance of 50 millionths of an inch, and was one-third the size of other machine tools performing the same work. The drill could be manually-fed or power-fed and was built for easy set-ups.

23 *SMU*, 30 March 1957, 1; 4 December 1957, 6; 24 March 1964, 1. Van Norman's demise was remarkably similar to Burgmaster, detailed by Holland, *When the Machine Stopped*. Holland notes that in the 1960s, because of high profits and seeming hold on the domestic market, US builders were enticing to conglomerates. He estimates that two-thirds of the industry was affected with the result that 'A distant managerial capitalism replaced entrepreneurial capitalism . . . ' p. 266.

24 Information on J&L gathered during a May 2001 interview in Springfield, Vermont with Faye Kingsbury, who retired from the company in the 1970s after working there for over 40 years, first as an apprentice machinist. Roe, *English and American Tool Builders*, ch. XV. For a history through the 1950s of the Springfield Vermont machine tool industry see Wayne Broehl, *Precision Valley: The Machine Tool Companies of Springfield Vermont* (Englewood Cliff, 1959).

25 Michael Gabriele, 'Goldman, building a machine tool empire', *Metalworking News*, 15 August 1988, 1; Arthur J. Alexander, 'Adaptation to Change in the US Machine Tool Industry', in Hong W. Tan and Haruo Shimada Kingsbury, eds, *Troubled Industries in the United States and Japan* (New York, 1994), pp. 321–367, 333; interview with Faye Kingsbury; interview with Jim Halvorsen in June 2001 at the American Precision Museum in Windsor, Vermont. Halvorsen was a manager at the Bryant Grinding Company for much of the 1970s and early 1980s. Little research has been done on the decline of Vermont firms. The American Precision Museum in Windsor, Vermont has many records from these companies. In mid 2001 production at J&L, Bryant, and Fellows Gear Shaper – all now owned by the Goldman Group – was consolidated in one wing of the Bryant factory.

26 Holland, *When the Machine Stopped*; Artemis March, *The US Machine Tool Industry and its Foreign Competitors* (Cambridge, MA, 1990).

27 Halvorsen interview, June 2001; Broehl, *Precision Valley*, pp. 184–89.

28 Kingsbury interview, June 2001. During other research efforts I have interviewed the owners of close to one hundred tool and die and precision metalworking firms in Western Massachusetts, most of which employ under 50 workers. There was a common response when I discussed with them the fact that a goodly number of their machine tools were foreign made, mostly from Japan: 'We needed the equipment right away and we needed decent service. US firms could promise neither of these things'.

29 Halvorsen and Kingsbury interviews. Gerry Khermouch, 'Vermont USA shifts focus, turns profit', *Metalworking News*, 3 September 1990, p. 6; 'Bridgeport, Conn., Machines Firm, Parent Seek Bankruptcy Protection', *The Connecticut Post*, 16 February 2002, p. 9.

30 Wagoner, *The US Machine Tool Industry*, p. 327.

31 CTI, *The Decline of the US Machine-Tool Industry*, p. 22; Anderson Ashburn, 'The Machine Tool Industry: The Crumbling Foundation', in Donald Hicks, ed., *Is New Technology Enough?* (Washington, DC, 1990), pp. 19–85, 80–81. In 1978, 40% of US machines in use were over 20 years old, while in Japan the figure was 18 percent. See Artemis March, *The US Machine Tool Industry and its Foreign Competitors*; NRC, *The US Machine Tool Industry*.

32 US builders paid scant attention to Japan builders' efforts to develop a range of exportable, stand-alone low-cost N/C machines appropriate for the

hundreds of small shops in Japan and the US. *American Machinist*, 1 June 1959.

33 Ashburn, 'The Machine Tool Industry'. MIT's engineers attempted to develop a universal system capable of commanding a machine tool to cut any mathematically definable contour. This required the development of what MIT engineers called 'continuous path NC'. For NC development in Great Britain see Ross Hamilton, 'Early British Machine Tool Automation: The Road to Numerical Control', *Journal of Industrial History* 2 (1999), pp. 96–121. Holland, *When the Machine Stopped*, p. 284; David Noble, *Forces of Production: A Social History of Industrial Automation* (New York, 1986). Hamilton contends that in the US it was necessary for the Air Force to create an artificial demand for the first N/C systems because the machine tool industry was 'notoriously conservative and unwilling to invest in the research and development of new technologies' p. 99. Similarly, British NC developers were hampered by a slow uptake in purchases.

34 For a discussion of numerical controls projects in the US in the 1950s see the study in *Control Engineering* published in three successive issues January – March 1958. There is no hint in the study that the systems being built were compatible. Surely this caused confusion among customers considering how to integrate the technology on their shop-floors. I am indebted to historian Philip Scranton for alerting me to the study.

35 Ashburn, 'The Machine Tool Industry', p. 48; Noble, *Forces of Production*.

36 David Hounshell, 'Automation, Transfer Machinery, and Mass Production', *Enterprise and Society* 1 (2000), pp. 100–138. Hounshell notes that transfer machinery makers 'experienced difficulties in effectively penetrating non-automotive, non-engine plant markets' p. 114; Holland, *When the Machine Stopped*, pp. 34–5.

37 Ashburn, 'The Machine Tool Industry', p. 49.

38 Holland, *When the Machine Stopped*, p. 34–5; Ashburn, 'The Machine Tool Industry', pp. 47–8; Bryn Jones, *Forging the Factory of the Future: Cybernation and Societal Institutions* (Cambridge, UK, 1997), esp. ch. 4; Bo Carlsson, 'The Development and Use of Machine Tools in Historical Perspective', in Richard Day and Gunner Eliasson, eds, *The Dynamics of Market Economies* (New York, 1986), pp. 247–69.

39 Masatsugu Tsuji, Makoto Ishikawa and Mineo Ishikawa, *Technology Transfer and Management in East Asian Machine Tool Industries: Lessons Learned From the Japanese Machine Tool Industry* (Osaka, 1996). Japanese firms that benefited from the agreements include Mitsubishi Heavy Industries, Toshiba Machine Company and Toyoda Machine Works. US firms involved include Burgmaster, Van Norman, Kearney & Trecker, Warner Swasey and Bryant. Between 1952 and 1981, when the law was repealed, there were 161 foreign technology licensing agreements. Ventures with US firms included: Koyo and Van Norman for centreless grinders; Toshiba Machine and Kearney & Trecker for transfer machines; and Sansei and Bryant for centreless grinders. Countries with the most agreements were the US with 67, West Germany with 33, and France with 32 (Toshiaki Chokki, 'A History of the Machine Tool Industry in Japan', in Martin Fransman, ed., *Machinery and Economic Development* (New York, 1986), pp. 124–52.

40 Burgmaster made an agreement in 1962 with Chukyo Denki, a Nagoya-based machine tool firm, giving the company rights to build and sell Burgmaster-designed machines in Asia. Burgmaster received a one-time payment for the engineering designs and annual royalties on sales. On these arrangements see Holland, *When the Machine Stopped*, pp. 48, 122–4. David Collis, *Kingsbury Machine Tool Corporation* (Boston, 1988), p. 7.

41 FANUC started as a division of electronics giant Fujitsu and competed with several US firms, including General Electric, Bendix, Sperry UMAC, and Actron in the development of machine tool controls. It was a 1972 spin-off from Fujitsu. In the early 1970s Bendix still owned all the basic NC patents and firms licensed the technology from Bendix at a cost of $500,000 – $1,000,000 per license. See CTI, *The Decline*, vol. 2, p. 108.

42 March, *The US Machine Tool Industry*, p. 5.

43 Michael Mealey, 'NC and Computers Build NC', *World Manufacturing* (November, 1974), pp. 31–4; Robert S. Eckley, *Global Competition in Capital Goods: An American Perspective* (New York, 1991), p. 123.

44 All data from the US Department of Commerce *Manufacturing Census*. The census is published by the US Government Printing Office and is carried out at five-year intervals. There are separate national and state reports. Contained in the state reports, is county-level and in some cases city-level data on manufacturing activity.

45 Wagoner, *The US Machine Tool Industry*, p. 327.

46 Ashburn, 'The Machine Tool Industry', p. 80; NRC, *The US Machine Tool Industry and the Defense Industrial Base*, pp. 14–15.

47 Ashburn, 'The Machine Tool Industry', p. 53.

48 Ashburn, 'The Machine Tool Industry', p. 81.

49 CTI, *The Decline of the US Machine-Tool Industry*, p. 65; March, *The US Machine Tool Industry*, pp. 12, 106–7. This disregard for exports dated back to the early twentieth century. As one industry historian concluded, US builders' interest in foreign markets 'appears to have varied inversely to the level of domestic demand' (Wagoner, *The United States Machine Tool Industry*, p. 227).

50 Department of Commerce, *Federal Manufacturing Census 1987* (Washington, DC, 1990).

51 NRC, *The US Machine Tool Industry and the Defense Industrial Base*.

52 William Corcoran, 'The Machine Tool Industry under Fire', in Donald Losman and Shu-Jan Liang, eds, *The Promise of American Industry: An Alternative Assessment of Problems and Prospects* (New York, 1990), pp. 227–47, 239.

53 Using Manufacturing Census data and reports from the NMTBA Ashburn determined that in the mid 1980s all types of NC were accounting for almost half the US consumption of machine tools and more than 60% of the NC machines were being imported. US-built NC horizontal lathes shipped rose from 1295 to 2230 between 1982 and 1987. However, NC vertical turning machines shipped declined from an anemic 194 machines to a microscopic 96 machines and NC machining centres declined to 1361 from 1396. Ashburn, 'The Machine Tool Industry', 1990, p. 5; CTI, *The Decline of the US Machine Tool Industry*, vol. 1, p. 15, vol. 2, pp. 5, 13, 104; March, *US Machine Tool Industry*.

54 NMTBA, *Meeting the Japanese Challenge*, p. 12.
55 March, *US Machine Tool Industry*, p. 15.
56 According to the National Research Council custom design requests diverted scarce engineering and management time to the construction of machine tools that 'will not be useful to other machine tool customers' (NRC, *The US Machine Tool Industry*, p. 67).
57 NMTBA, *Meeting the Japanese Challenge*, pp. 12–13.
58 CTI, *The Decline of the US Machine Tool Industry*, vol. 1, p. 49. For a discussion of the German apprenticeship system and the importance of skill see vol. 2 of the CTI study, esp. pp. 28–35. The Pratt & Whitney quote is from a 1945 sales catalog in the company's file at the American Precision Museum.
59 *UE News*, 'Local 218 Keeps Jobs in Springfield, Vermont', UE News Archives, www. ranknfile-ue. org/uen; Greg Gatlin, 'Machine tool firm files for Chapter 11', *The Boston Herald*, 20 February 2002, p. 31.

Index

Printed in the United States
by Baker & Taylor Publisher Services